'Did you think contentment
life, something beyond your control? Dr Pam Spurr is
here to put you in charge, to give you the means to make
a choice; to be a little or a whole lot happier. Through
her 10 Happiness Principles, Dr Pam shows you what
you need to be happy and what you can do to bring, as
she puts it, the "three Es" – good emotions, experiences
and energy – into your life. This is a life-affirming and
life changing book – I highly recommend it!'

Suzie Hayman, agony aunt, author and Times *columnist*

HOW TO BE A HAPPY HUMAN

10 Essential Principles
to Change Your Life

Dr Pam Spurr

BOOKS

First published in Great Britain in 2010 by
JR Books, 10 Greenland Street, London NW1 0ND
www.jrbooks.com

ISBN 978-1-906779-31-3

1 3 5 7 9 10 8 6 4 2

Printed by CPI Bookmarque, Croydon, CR0 4TD

For Nick, Sam and Stephie: I love you all dearly – you're at the absolute heart of my happiness.

In memory of my late-mother and late-father: you filled my heart with happiness and I carry you with me every day.

For Chris, my mother-in-law: a wonderful woman with an infectious laugh.

To my three older brothers: thanks for the happy times – and all those to come.

To my friends: thanks for all the good times we share – you can count on me the way I've counted on you.

www.drpam.co.uk

Contents

Acknowledgements

With heartfelt thanks to the many, many people who have crossed my path and shared their stories with me. From those who've experienced at times profound unhappiness, to those who have at times reached the pinnacle of happiness – and in many cases those who have experienced both.

My warmest thanks go to Jeremy Robson and Lesley Wilson for their encouragement to write this book.

Foreword

Who is the book for?

I have based the 10 Happiness Principles to come on thousands of interviews and conversations with people about what increases their happiness or has brought them unhappiness. On the basis of these conversations, this book is for you if your own expectations of happiness and desire for a happy life have been jeopardised by having felt or because you now feel:

♦ emotionally needy, helpless, hopeless, a fake or a phoney, over-driven to succeed, stuck in a rigid routine, a tendency to 'beat yourself up', a lack of self-belief, a belief that you're not as 'good as' others around you.

♦ an inability to forge loving relationships, that you have dysfunctional relationships, are undermined/undervalued in relationships both personally and at work.

♦ taken for granted, feeling bullied, and you're not good enough to receive love.

♦ overwhelmed by stress, out of control, experiencing bouts of anxiety, having destructive phobias and fears, loneliness, self-critical or overly critical of others, or any other state of being that you'd describe as unhappy.

How To Be A Happy Human will show you another way of feeling and being.

This book is also for you if you've ever experienced or right now feel:

◆ happiness, *un*happiness that you've come to understand, joy, contentment, confidence, valued, worthy, successful, appreciated and/or appreciative, needed, optimistic, positive, excited, creative, generally blessed or any other state of being you'd describe as happy.

How To Be A Happy Human will enhance these and ensure they continue.

A word of caution

If you suffer from depression or any serious mental illness I'm heartened that you're reading *How to be a Happy Human* as I'm sure there'll be strategies and suggestions that will help you even in small ways. However I most strongly advise you to see your doctor as you may need counselling, medication or both to help you heal and that's something *How to be a Happy Human* cannot provide.

Introduction

Welcome to *How to be a Happy Human*. I'd guess there are two main reasons – and probably a million in between them – why you've decided to pick up my book: because on the whole you consider yourself to be a fairly happy person but at times question whether you could be happier; or because you've experienced anything from regular bouts of unhappiness to a great deal of unhappiness, and you know that a happier life awaits you.

I *know* that you can become a happy – or happier – human. I know this from my own experience and that of others. I have seen the various changes people can make in their behaviour, feelings, expectations and life generally, when they decide they want to be happier. They've demonstrated they can have amazing success in taking control and making the right changes, and gaining understanding into their unhappiness – and that transforms their lives.

But making the right changes and adopting the right attitudes isn't like a magic wand that you wave and suddenly you find that your life is happier. If that was the case then miraculously overnight all of us would be happier humans. I'm not going to feed you a sugar-coated fantasy that you're going to end up happy every minute of every day of your life. No, the changes I know you can make and I've seen so many people make, including myself, require some thought and effort. But the journey in doing these things is rewarding in itself. Because one thing we forget in the way we live today is that we, as humans, were meant to be challenged – not by something that could be considered a hollow victory like learning how to use the latest piece of technology, but in meaningful ways through self-discovery. To discover who you really are and what you're really like – and ultimately what makes you happy.

Some of the changes I'll suggest – and I've seen people make – apply to the majority of people's lives, and that includes your life. With a little bit of effort and with the right strategies and suggestions such changes are completely do-able and obtainable. Other changes in behaviour and feelings, attitudes and choices, are unique to the individual who is making them so they can be happier within their own unique life. We can still learn from their stories and I'll include many such stories throughout the coming chapters.

Where it's relevant I'll be honest with you in *How to be a Happy Human* and tell you about changes I've made to became happier, as well as showing you the insights others have discovered, often through trial and error, and adopted to gain happiness. I'm certainly not alone in having experienced unhappiness – I suspect you have too – and research confirms that presently we humans are experiencing high levels of stress, anxiety and depression that stops us from being happy.[1]

The Happiness Principles

I'm also writing this book based on a vast sea of experience: the thousands of people I've professionally and personally had the pleasure and privilege to meet, talk to, or correspond with about the happiness and unhappiness they feel. It's staggering when hearing the stories of so many different people, from various walks of life, that even though each of their individual tales is different in detail, they still distill into a number of common principles – the **Happiness Principles**, as I call them. These determine their levels of happiness or unhappiness.

People don't realise as they tell their story about being happy or unhappy, or of a happy or unhappy time, that what they describe almost always fits into the themes covered in the forthcoming Happiness Principles. There are common threads to their stories; it's simply the details and their individual reactions that are different.

I hope you'll seize the Happiness Principles as I introduce them chapter by chapter and make them part of your everyday life. These are the main principles that govern our happiness and can change our unhappiness. Absorb them, use them and reclaim or develop happiness in your life. There are 10 Happiness Principles covering major themes that are central to increasing your levels of happiness and understanding any unhappiness. The principles range from the profound, like why you might fill a painful emotional 'hole' in your heart with alcohol, to the simple, such as why you should treasure yourself each and every day. They range from the serious, like how your parents might influence your happiness *even when you're an adult* to the practical, like how to face and overcome fears you have that hold you back from happiness.

Some of my Happiness Principles cover more ground and go into more depth than others, which are covered by briefer passages. You may at times think, 'Why can't Pam spend more time on this area?', particularly when you can identify yourself in a passage and know that it applies directly to your levels of happiness. You might find that frustrating and want more analysis and information. However, there's so much to cover in the tremendous, important and changing landscape of our happiness as humans that I've had to be selective. I've included so many different and relevant thoughts, themes and concepts that I've simply had to crack on through some of them. Where I feel it's necessary I've spent more time on others. I will have done my job if I've stimulated you to want more information and think further about some of these.

Just as you may wish for more analysis on one particular area, there may be others that you think don't apply to you and your life. At first glance it's easy to brush something off as irrelevant to you. But if you take a moment to consider such passages you may find it's more relevant to your life than you'd think. Don't close your mind and jump the gun thinking you can skip a particular passage, as you may miss out on something valuable to your happiness.

If from chapter headings you see one further on in the book and you think, 'Ah-ha, that's completely relevant to me!' please resist the urge to skip ahead, and instead read through each chapter in turn.

Also, in each chapter I develop the relevant theme building up to that chapter's specific Happiness Principle. So please don't expect it to be revealed at the start of each chapter.

How to be a Happy Human isn't going to be a passive read. No, there's much for you to do. So I hope that where I ask you to put pen to paper, you'll take a moment to do so. Throughout the book you may find you need more space to write down your thoughts.

You could try keeping a notebook handy for these sections. It can be surprising how making a note to yourself, about something personal to your life, can help clarify it. By 'thinking in ink' you're more likely to have 'lightbulb' moments of revelation and understanding. It's worth your time and effort.

I know you may be extremely keen to get stuck straight into the Happiness Principles and all the strategies, tips and techniques I'll describe for you to try. First there are a few thoughts I'd like to consider briefly before we get down to the business of showing you that change is possible when it comes to you and your way of dealing with the world, and how this may hold you back from, or enhance, your happiness.

As well as being based largely on the stories of thousands of people, *How to be a Happy Human* is also based on research that I'll mention from time to time. This is research into what makes people happy or unhappy in different areas of their lives. Why some seem to enjoy more happiness or happy times *consistently* in their lives, and why for others happiness is an elusive dream. This research is important, particularly at this time, as generally speaking we live in a fairly unhappy era and it was way back in the 1950s that we were at our happiest.[2] **Please note that you can use any of the strategies and ideas that might apply to you from any of the personal stories throughout *How to be a Happy Human*.**

Just what is happiness?

You may think that it's time for me to define happiness. We could take a loose dictionary definition that it's a state of well-being, contentment and pleasure. But what does that really tell us? What makes one person happy won't necessarily have the same effect in another. Also, the intensity of that well-being, contentment and pleasure varies tremendously between people and between situations. There are big, long, curling threads of happiness that run through people's lives as well as momentary and fleeting feelings of joy.

Rather than worry about definitions, I think it's important that you recognise in yourself when you feel that uplifting emotion, that certain type of contentment or satisfaction – *and enjoy it*. You can distinguish between your own emotional states: when you feel happy, when you feel unhappy, and the various points in between. You know that magical moment when you forget everything else apart from the joy you have in your heart. *Happy Human* is about learning to enhance what's at the root of such positive emotional states, and understanding what decreases your chances of happiness – in other words what brings unhappiness into your life.

The importance of unhappiness

Speaking of unhappiness, I'd like to make another key and important point before we go any further: I'm not saying unhappiness is a bad thing! In fact, on the whole, it's a positive thing. In order to embrace genuine happiness you need to understand the other side of the coin – unhappiness. There's no such thing as a life that escapes all unhappiness. No matter how blessed your life seems, you'll have to face life's hurdles and challenges, and these may cause you unhappiness. What's important is learning to understand it, knowing how to roll with the punches, exploring solutions, finding the power to overcome it, and taking preventative action with future happiness in mind.

Think of periods of unhappiness as a great opportunity! An opportunity to learn about yourself and discover important things, like how you might have done something differently, or reacted differently to a situation, what works for you and what doesn't.

A word of warning if you've experienced a great deal of unhappiness: please don't look to those who always seem to be happy as an example of what you hope to be like. As we shall see, those who claim always to be happy are usually hiding behind a façade of happiness. It isn't real. Often, behind their façade, they're terribly unhappy. Usually they fear that if they don't put on this 'front' they will be unacceptable in some way. Perhaps they feel they will burden others if they admit they're unhappy about something. Or they may even fear they will be seen as unlovable if they're unhappy. They begin to believe it's better to keep up the happy front rather than risk finding out that others don't think they're worth supporting through unhappy periods.

I personally know how the depths of unhappiness make us appreciate happiness when we have it. I recognise the power we have inside us to understand our unhappiness, roll with it, and change it even if at first we don't realise we have that power. I was so profoundly unhappy during my divorce in the early 1990s that deep down I worried I'd never fully recover to be the person I tend to be: a happy human. The root of my unhappiness was that I feared my precious children would be hurt by the divorce, which in turn made me feel like a failure. All I wanted at the time was to be the best possible mother I could be and to protect them from the repercussions of the divorce. Interestingly – and this is how emotions like happiness can work – it was the power of the happiness I had from my role as mother that helped me through. Although it was a long and winding road, I came out the other side. I faced my unhappiness down – much of which was due to that sense of having failed my children. Eventually I realised that it wasn't 'failing them' to actually provide them with a happier home life.

Have I *always* been happy since that point? No, of course not, and as I hope you'll soon see, it wouldn't be human to always be happy. I do, though, treasure the happiness that comes my way or that I create in my life. No matter what the hurdle is I know that I can rely on my sheer 'will' to face it and on the power of happiness along the way to carry me through – be it spontaneous happy moments, or the essential happiness in, say, my relationships. Happiness is a powerful emotion.

Why do we even have emotions if they're going to be challenging?

Why would we be given these emotions, like unhappiness and happiness, that can be so complicated and challenging? Humans evolved a variety of emotional states that set them apart in the animal world. Emotions developed to give our ancient ancestors a message that they needed to take some sort of action about a situation. At a practical level this means that when something makes you happy you take action simply to enjoy this feelgood emotion, to prolong it if possible, and do more of the thing that brought you the happiness in the first place. Or if something makes you unhappy, you need to act on that negative emotion and do something about its cause to (hopefully) get rid of it.

Emotions are complex and go hand-in-hand with the complexities of our mind. Just try to describe an emotion in a few words – it's hard! Also it becomes a more complex picture when you realise that, frequently, different emotions, from different events, are competing for your attention at the same time. Here's an easy example: you receive a loving call from your partner in the middle of the day saying how much he/she cares for you. As you hang up the phone your boss walks in and criticises a report you've written. You have a warm, feelgood emotion on the one hand, competing with emotions of anger and frustration on the other. Which do you pay attention to? The happy, warm emotion, or the unhappy, frustrating emotion? Well, that all depends on you, your personality and how much you naturally live your life by the Happiness Principles that I know to be important.

Research confirms this[3] – the importance we allocate to each different emotion has a lot to do with our basic personality traits. Also, it's a fact that once our attention is allocated to one competing emotion or another, this simple act (of where we allocate our attention) helps determine our overall level of happiness. So if you regularly choose to pay more attention to your angry, sad or frustrated emotional responses than to your happy ones, that will help determine your overall level of happiness – or in this case, your unhappiness. It's that old 'cup half-full or half-empty' divide.

Overall the impact of having complex emotions gives us the opportunity to experience life at an enriched and more varied level. As our emotions grew more complex, so too did human society grow increasingly complex. This complexity has interesting repercussions for our levels of happiness and I absolutely believe that the growing complexity of life, over the last two decades particularly, has done some damage to our potential to be happy. I'll look at this in more detail in Chapter Ten.

Time will tell

Take a moment to look at your watch now and note down the time.

Now think about the last time you felt happy – when was it and what were you doing? Next, take a look at the time again and see how long it took for you to recall a happy memory. How many seconds, or minutes, even, did it take?

If your answer is longer than a few seconds, then I can tell you right now, you need to bring more happiness into your life.

HAPPY FACT: *It only takes 12 muscles to smile, so exercise them!*

So what do humans need to be happy?

As we shall see there are many different things that influence why we are happy or unhappy and when. These things include themes like understanding ourselves, taking charge of our life, appreciating what we have, not being pressured by others to live a certain way, seizing moments, taking opportunities and much, much more. They form the basis for the Happiness Principles. We'll now turn to these to see the part they play in human happiness. You will be able to decide how each fits into your life, as well as putting into action the recommended strategies and solutions that will lead you to more happiness.

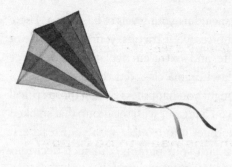

In the Beginning . . .

*Life's greatest happiness is to be convinced
we are loved.*

Victor Hugo

One of the biggest questions we ask ourselves that relates to our core happiness or unhappiness is: How did I come to be the person that I am today? The person that either enjoys a fair amount of happiness, maybe even lots of happiness, or has known a great deal of unhappiness? What shaped you to be the sort of person who feels they are loved – and worthy of happiness – or perhaps the person who is convinced they are unloved and maybe feels unworthy of happiness? One part of the answer lies in your childhood and the parenting you've received.

I say 'one part' of the answer, because although your parents have an enormous influence on you in your early life, as you get older increasingly other influences start to make an impact on who you are and how you feel, including your levels of happiness. These influences include your choices, your friends, your larger circle of relations, your school life and extra-curricular activities. For instance, in your after-school drama class did you discover a real love for the stage that brought you happiness during those critical adolescent years? Or did you hang out with the group that smoked behind the bike sheds, and get into trouble with your teachers, which led to lots of rows with your parents? All such decisions influence your life and your happiness.

Moving on, influences other than your parents include those you meet in further education and your work life, plus all the other people you come into contact with and the experiences you have. However we can't get around the fact that your parents are the most significant influence in shaping who you are – and your well-being and enjoyment of life – for a good part of your first 18 or so years.

In fact, how you were parented and how that influences your well-being is an important topic worthy of a book all of its own. In the light of that, my purpose with the first Happiness Principle, to come in this chapter, is to highlight a key issue – the 'blame game' – that can potentially emerge from your childhood. As we shall see this issue can have a tremendous effect on your levels of happiness. I say 'potentially', as not all of us experience this key issue; however it's important we are aware of it so that it doesn't undermine our happiness in any other shape or form.

What if you had wonderful parents?

Another important point to make is that even if you were blessed with wonderful parents who nurtured, loved and protected you, the thoughts, ideas and strategies in this chapter will probably be relevant to you in other aspects of your life. They aren't just relevant to those who have experienced less-than-good parenting. The key issue of the blame game, to be highlighted below, may come into play in different situations, so this chapter may be thought-provoking and helpful whatever the quality of the parent–child relationship you experienced.

Over one hundred years ago, Sigmund Freud pointed out how important in particular the first five years of life were in terms of the development of your personality: the essence of who you are. What foresight he had! Other research has since pointed out additional key phases in the further development and crystallisation of your personality, as in the pre-teens (the tweenies) and adolescence. A big part of what happens to you, and how you are treated from birth onwards, helps to determine how happy you are later in life.

This is because, as your personality is shaped in childhood, various traits get 'expressed' such as being relaxed or excitable, serious or silly, bookish or sports-mad, etc. But your personality also includes things like how positive you are, how flexible you are, how prepared you are to see the 'upside' of a situation, and such things account for much of the happiness you will enjoy.

Interestingly your genetic heritage also accounts for some aspects of your happiness. Recent research shows that perhaps around 50 per cent of one trait relating to happiness – having a 'happy outlook' – is down to our genes[4]. Essentially what this means is that there's a real interaction between nature and nurture, and that you get a double whammy from your parents. Not only do you inherit from them some aspects of your potential to be happy – so if your father was a grumpy old so-and-so, you may end up like that too – but you also get from parents the effects of how they raised you and that influences whether you enjoy and experience more or less happiness.

But before you think something like, 'Well, as my dad was grumpy, and I am too, then there's nothing I can do about it, I guess I'll never be very happy', I have a view for you – I firmly believe you can improve on what you think you might have inherited. Your will is stronger than your nature. So your will to be happy can overcome what might be part of your nature. And other research confirms this.

 HAPPY FACT: *Happiness is contagious – research shows you're 30 times more likely to feel happy in public than when you're on your own!*

Until it's pointed out to them, people often don't understand how their parents, and their parents' parenting skills, have such an impact on them in the here-and-now once they've grown up. This is usually due to the simple fact that they just don't associate how their parents treated them as children with repercussions for the future. However much the parenting you received affects you now, I firmly believe that no matter what you've received from your parents in terms of nature and nurture, you have the power to create and embrace happiness. More on that later, but to help make this point about our parents and their profound long-term influence on our well-being, let's think of the impact others have on our happiness. I'll use an example from romantic relationships and the lasting effect they can have on your well-being.

If you've ever had a painful break-up you'll understand what I'm talking about. When you've been hurt by someone you've loved, one of the most common reactions I come across is that of *mistrust* – particularly mistrust of potential partners, as and when they happen to cross your path in future. This mistrust can persist for quite a long time, and along with mistrust comes unhappiness. So not only do you have the initial heartbreak, but then your reaction to it – mistrust of others – compounds it.

The cycle of mistrust

This feeling can become a self-fulfilling cycle of mistrust that can spin on and on in some people. It becomes a dysfunctional habit that cripples their potential to enjoy future relationships. And for some it only takes one experience of a broken heart to make them wary of how others might treat them – and whether they are willing to face more potential heartache. That in turn can make people hold back, or play games, or feel anxiety about a new potential partner in their life. All of these responses are part of the cycle of mistrust.

Your emotional resilience

Let's say that before the break-up you might have had some good experiences with relationships. You might have had great and lasting friendships. You might have had a manager or boss who treated you well and showed you respect. And you might have had previous romantic relationships where they ran their natural course so you weren't all that hurt by them coming to an end. Of all these experiences of relationships that could potentially influence your levels of trust in others, which is the one that influences your levels of trust, at least initially after the break-up? *It's the painful heartbreak.* How long for, though, depends on your emotional resilience.

Now let's rewind back to your childhood. If you had a parent who was inconsistent with you, or seemed to prefer your brother or sister, was overly harsh with you, or hurt you – or any other type of mistreatment – that's what you'll most likely hold onto and take into future situations, even if you're not aware of it. This is because, on the whole, painful experiences seem to affect us in a 'once bitten, twice shy' type of way. And we might develop this cycle of mistrust even when it comes to our parents. If we have lots of painful experiences in our youth, then they establish all sorts of negative attitudes in us like the cycle of mistrust, as well as negative beliefs and behaviour in our future dealings with life – including whether or not we allow ourselves to be happy.

Depending on your previous experiences, though, you might more easily break this cycle of mistrust because of your emotional resilience. Largely, your emotional resilience depends on how many positive experiences you've had, *in balance with* how many negative experiences you've had. The more positive emotional experiences you have, the less profound the effect that negative emotional experiences will have on you. Think of your emotional resilience like a balancing scale that tips in one direction or another – positively or negatively. Those people with more emotional resilience bounce back quicker and enjoy more happiness.

Thinking of that romantic example again, with good emotional resilience you may be willing to test the romantic waters sooner and seek out future happiness with another person. The good news for some is that if you've had a bad break-up, as in this example, but you also have emotional resilience, it gives you reserves of trust, happy experiences, feeling loved, etc. Then any mistrust you feel goes away more quickly and you're able to move on and look forward positively to meeting new potential partners in future.

It's the same with the influence your parents have on your future happiness. The more equilibrium you experienced as a child with them, the more emotional resilience you developed, and the easier it is to overcome the times when they were, say, angry at you. Believe me, even the best, most patient and well-intentioned parents can sometimes take things out on their children. There isn't one single person who hasn't experienced as a child having their parents act badly on occasion, even if on the whole they were great parents. Parents are only human. So at times when they're incredibly stressed or overwhelmed by something, it's their child who may be on the receiving end of a bad temper or a 'telling off' that wasn't justifiable. But if that child has experienced good parenting *on the whole* from their parents – and developed good emotional resilience – then a little setback like that isn't going to spoil their ability to experience happiness, both then and in the future. As children they won't move into a cycle of mistrust, but will move quickly out of it and trust their parents again.

When a child receives poor parenting and experiences many emotional setbacks, it's almost understandable that they end up mistrusting their parents, and others they come into contact with. Unfortunately when this happens it often leads to a child that grows up into an adult who points the finger of blame, saying, *'They've* made me the way I am, they've made me unhappy.' We'll explore this key issue of the 'blame game' in a moment. Also in Chapter Five we'll take a closer look at breaking the cycle of mistrust. But first I'd like to remind you of the extraordinary drive and determination found in your will.

The power of your will

I'll come back to this theme many times in *Happy Human* as this is a message that I hope you will absorb, and reabsorb: that you hold a huge amount of power in your will. If you have the will to leave behind any mistrustful, sad or angry feelings about the way you were raised – and how you think that influences how you feel now – you can make changes to do so. Of course if you compare yourself to someone you know who received much love and understanding in their childhood, you may feel it's a much tougher task to start enjoying as much happiness as they might do. And that may be true. But you can't let that comparison hold you back – your will exists to conquer such things.

The parenting you received

Before we go further, take a moment to write down here two words (for example, strict, kind, anxious) that describe the way your mother parented you.

✎ ....

Now write down here two words (for example, strict, kind, anxious) that describe the way your father parented you.

✎ ....

Now write down here two memories from childhood to do with your parents – one happy and one unhappy.

✎ ....

✎ ....

Next answer this question: considering your unhappy memory, with hindsight can you now understand why your parents acted as they did?

The blame game

This brings me to the key issue you must consider in terms of your own happiness as an adult. This issue is the 'blame game' as applied to your parents and the way you feel *now*. Sadly, many unhappy adults get caught up in a blame game that they can never, ever win. A blame game where every day that they feel unhappy, or every time they don't feel good about themselves, they think, 'It's all because of my mum – she never treated me well, that's why I'm like this!' Or 'It's all because of my dad – he was never around, he didn't care about me, how can I ever be happy?' Or they may believe that both of their parents have made them the unhappy person they are today because neither parent was good to them.

It's quite natural when you feel bad, when life feels as if it's always a challenge, when you don't have much hope, you feel mistrustful, and things don't feel very happy, to want to blame someone. The natural fallback, or default position, is to blame your parents – particularly because there's so much in the media, in books, or on TV programmes about how parents affect their children. It's easy to say, 'See, it must be my parents' fault I feel this way!' But by pointing the finger of blame you never take responsibility for your own happiness *now* as an adult.

Forgiveness

If you feel you were let down by your parents and that perhaps they didn't show you the warmth and love you would have liked – forgive them. As I'll discuss in coming paragraphs, they may not have known any better. They may have felt they were doing their best. Forgiveness is a 'bridging act' that can cross the divide from the past and make your present happier. There are circumstances where forgiveness may be impossible or inappropriate, as in the case where a parent was particularly abusive (emotionally, physically and/or sexually) to their child.

Of course you can finger-point at your parents for the rest of your life and use them as a reason why you can never feel happy. You can tell yourself that because of them you don't trust others. Just as the person with a broken heart decides it's easier to keep blaming their ex who hurt them for their continued unhappiness – and the cycle of mistrust they've landed in – it's the same with long-standing unhappiness and blaming your parents. In fact it's almost easier to blame your parents for ongoing unhappiness in life than to actually grab life by the throat and decide you're going to make more of it. Ultimately playing the blame game will keep you stuck in unhappiness as Deborah was (see overleaf).

Deborah's unhappy story

Think about how it would feel to believe your parents didn't really want you to be happy, or had such a restricted view of life that it crushed your happiness. Those are the sorts of feelings Deborah had.

Deborah, 33, is a single teacher living in a large city. When I met this attractive but serious-looking brunette, Deborah was finding it a hard slog to get up every day and go into the school where she taught biology. Where once upon a time she felt she could make a real difference in teaching, that feeling had long since gone. Deborah hadn't been out with anybody since her mid-20s and was extremely lonely. She often sat in her small flat on her own at night slumped in front of the television, sipping more wine than she probably should throughout the evening.

The next day at work she'd pretend to her colleagues that she'd been out with friends the night before. She would occasionally fib and invent a fictional man and make up having dates with him. To keep her cover story in place she would always say that things had fizzled out when a colleague would ask her about 'that new man'. Deborah felt she had to keep up this pretence or risk colleagues judging her as a sad singleton.

Even when she had dated in the past she'd never really felt loved by her boyfriends or cared for in the way she imagined someone luckier, or more deserving, would be. This downward spiral continued as Deborah pretended to colleagues that she was OK, and yet increasingly her evenings were spent alone with only a bottle of wine for comfort and company.

Deborah was an only child and by this time rarely saw her parents. When she thought of her parents she'd get quite angry and down. She felt they'd been overly strict with her as she was growing up due to the fact that she was a poorly child. She felt they'd never let her 'do anything or go anywhere', and that made her feel different from her classmates while growing up. As with having had some experience of boyfriends, she did also have friends when she was at university but they all seemed to fall by the wayside. If truth be told Deborah never felt she was quite as good as anyone else and this included friends, boyfriends and colleagues. She blamed this on the way her parents raised her in a bit of a bubble, through being overly cautious and strict. She thought it had affected her personality, meaning that people didn't find her very appealing.

When Deborah did occasionally visit her parents it was all a bit strained. She arrived on their doorstep for a planned weekend feeling fairly optimistic and hoping it would be 'lovely'. But she always left at the end of the weekend with a feeling of, 'What was the point of that? All mum and dad did was go on about me not having a boyfriend.'

Over the last couple of years these visits became harder as she increasingly blamed her parents for the general unhappiness she felt. Deborah had gone her longest time yet of 10 months without seeing them, due to a row she'd had with them the last time she'd visited. It began with her mother saying that Deborah was 'moping around the place' and that she'd 'never get a boyfriend with such a long face'. The fury that erupted from Deborah shocked and surprised her parents. They had a terrible row where Deborah accused them of not wanting her to be happy and of raising her in a way that had made her an emotional cripple. She also blamed them for the fact she'd 'never find happiness'.

It was clear when Deborah told her story that she was bound up in the blame game, feeling her parents still held the key to her happiness *right now* in her life – even as a 33-year-old. It was obvious she was literally chained to her past and her view that her parents had made her past unhappy . . . *and so it continued today.*

Deborah's happy beginning

Deborah needed to wake up quickly to the reality that regardless of how her parents might have raised her, she was now responsible for her own happiness and well-being. How did she turn her perspective around and accept responsibility for herself? Deborah tried a number of strategies, including the following.

Truthful listening: Deborah needed to undertake some truthful listening to begin to acknowledge the blame game she played with her parents. She recorded herself speaking into a dictaphone where she had to discuss her feelings towards her parents for three minutes. Three minutes was long enough to prove a point! When she analysed the content of what she said she was shocked by how much responsibility for her well-being she placed at her parents' door. She literally hadn't 'heard' her own voice in the past, but now it was crystal clear that she was jabbing a long finger of blame repeatedly at her mother and father. The truthful listening technique was profoundly helpful.

Self-responsibility strategy: When you've been holding someone else like your parents accountable for your happiness, you stop taking responsibility for it yourself. A technique that was going to help Deborah was to reclaim, throughout her life, responsibility for herself. It's easy once you play the blame game in one area of your life to let that slip into other areas. And when she explored this, this is exactly what Deborah found she had done, particularly in one area – friendships with work colleagues. When questioned why she never socialised with colleagues – many of whom she said were very likeable – Deborah said because *they* never asked *her* out. Or at least those who had initially asked her to meet up after work, when she first taught at school, had long since stopped. When asked to repeat her reasoning, because she'd already done the dictaphone technique talking about her parents, she actually 'heard' her voice putting the responsibility for going out with colleagues on to them. With this clearly in mind Deborah took it upon herself to make the first move to ask a couple of colleagues out socially.

Finding your 'guardian angel': A theme that emerged in conversations was that Deborah was very hard on herself – as well as playing the blame game with her parents. There was certainly no sense that there was anything from within her that was looking after or nurturing her. Her inner voice repeatedly told her that she wasn't a very interesting person, she wasn't particularly lovable, and so on. Deborah allowed this 'little devil' to sit on her shoulder and literally bring her mood down. It whipped up a cycle of anxious thinking that she'd never be able to find love or settle down with anyone. As she wanted more than anything to settle down with someone, by default this little devil of a voice talking in her ear meant that she'd never be happy. Deborah needed to coax along a kinder inner voice that would replace that little devil and be the guardian angel on her shoulder. On a little notepad she could easily carry around, Deborah made a note of when that little devil would start chattering and what the content of her thoughts, in the form of this chatter, were. After a few days she sat down and studied her notes. There in black and white was clear evidence of the negativity she carried around inside of her. Deborah was again surprised by what she herself was doing that jeopardised happiness. She began to talk back to her little devil and encourage a new guardian angel to speak to her. Deborah adopted a more soothing voice that said good things about her and helped to lighten her general mood.

These three techniques were critical for Deborah, changing her essential unhappiness to potential happiness. After what she'd learnt about herself Deborah grew savvier about how her outlook had tainted her chances of happiness. She realised how much the techniques had helped her take a fresh look at the choices she made that impacted on her well-being. As with any such technique it's important to revisit them from time to time to strengthen their effects and this is exactly what she did.

You might think Deborah's story is not such a big deal considering, say, that her parents weren't physically abusive, or that her father hadn't run off with another woman, and her mother wasn't a drunk. But I hope you'll come to recognise that it doesn't take anything that traumatic to have a lasting impact on your levels of happiness when you decide to play the blame game. It can only take something like overprotectiveness, or rigid attitudes towards a child, to leave people feeling that they can't let go and really enjoy life and find happiness. Believe me, there will be some rather more traumatic stories to come.

Ignorance is not bliss

On the one hand there are those like Deborah who repeatedly point the finger of blame at their parents for the way they feel now as adults. Then there are those people who fail to realise what a profound effect their childhood, and the parenting they received, has on their well-being or lack of it – today, in the here and now. In some ways it's equally unhelpful to walk around not knowing why you find it hard to enjoy happy moments when they come your way, or why you don't feel very good inside, making it hard to experience happiness.

People like this wonder where the impulses they have come from – for example, to reject love when it comes their way because they're not sure they want to get close to someone. They may feel they haven't a clue why they always see the downside of a situation even though they'd like to be more optimistic. They might wonder why they have certain personality traits that lead them straight down the path to unhappiness. These can be traits like, say, being arrogant and putting people off, making them feel that you don't want to know them, when actually you'd like to know them. Of course, this in turn means that they don't have the opportunity to share the sort of time with those they come across that could lead them down the path to happiness.

Such naivety about how they came to be the people they are – particularly if they are unhappy – is not helpful to moving on. Although you don't want to get trapped in the blame game as some do, equally, having a bit of insight about why you tick the way you tick can make an enormous difference. It can help you change your attitudes, responses to situations and behaviour that leads you towards unhappiness, and instead embrace those things that increase happiness.

It's now a good time to bring together the things I've said about the parenting you've received and what it means to your happiness *now*. The parenting you received may absolutely have a large effect on how you feel now but the key is whether it's a lasting effect, and whether it's negative or positive, and that's up to you.

Happiness Principle One

Regardless of your upbringing, you have the power to choose to find happiness.

In other words your happiness is shaped by the way you were raised – but that doesn't mean you can't change it. We are not slaves to our childhoods, but it's important to understand how the echoes from our childhoods reach forward throughout our lives – sometimes in the most profound ways.

With this first Happiness Principle in mind, it's the emotionally intelligent person who comes to realise two things:

♦ First, they realise that their parents had a profound impact on their life and the development of their personality plus the way they feel – and that includes the amount of happiness they feel. They are *not* ignorant of this fact.

♦ Second, they realise that no matter what sort of parenting they received – even poor or abusive parenting – they are the master or mistress of their own destiny and they will not allow that upbringing to damage their chances of happiness. They will *not* be ensnared by the blame game.

 How much impact did your parents have on your present happiness?

As with all quizzes throughout *Happy Human*, please answer each question honestly. You'll only be fooling yourself if you don't! If any answer doesn't exactly suit your situation, attitude or behaviour then please choose the answer that most resembles your situation, attitude or behaviour.

1. Do you ever find yourself blaming your parents for the way you feel now?

   🅐 Yes, frequently
   🅑 No, infrequently
   🅒 Sometimes

2. Do you ever 'hear' your mother/father's voice in your head, speaking to you in a negative way?

   🅐 Yes, definitely
   🅑 No, not at all
   🅒 Sometimes

3. When you think about the way your parents raised you, do you mainly have:

   🅐 Negative feelings?
   🅑 Positive feelings?
   🅒 A mix of negative and positive feelings?

4. When comparing yourself to others do you feel your upbringing was harder, more difficult, less happy, and so on, than theirs?

   🅐 Yes, definitely
   🅑 No, not at all
   🅒 In some ways yes, and in some ways no

5. Do you feel an inexplicable resentment towards your parents?

   🅐 Yes, I do
   🅑 No, I don't
   🅒 Sometimes I do

6. Do you mention in disagreements or arguments with your parents the 'negative/bad/unhappy way' you felt you were raised?

Ⓐ Yes, I do
Ⓑ No, I don't
Ⓒ Sometimes I do

Your responses

More than three 'A' answers
The blame game. You are playing the blame game and it's detrimental to your levels of happiness. As well as the techniques that Deborah used (and which might definitely benefit you), there are some solutions to this below.

Any 'A' answers at all
Some blame. If you chose even one 'A' answer, check out the advice below. Even one 'A' answer can mean that at critical moments you might choose to play the blame game and not take control of your own happiness.

More than four 'B' answers
Little or no blame. On the whole you accept responsibility for your life generally and your levels of happiness or unhappiness specifically. That's a very positive place to be. It's important to be aware that if there's friction with your parents, for any reason, you don't let this influence your well-being in the rest of your life.

More than three 'C' answers
Some blame. You veer between blaming your parents for some of the way your life is – and that includes your emotional states like how happy/unhappy you are – and accepting responsibility for the rest. Please see the advice below.

Don't play the blame game

Recognise faulty reasoning: Every time you find yourself blaming your parents for the way you feel, tell yourself that this is 'faulty reasoning'. Faulty reasoning stops you from facing life the way it is, accepting what you can do to change things about your situation, and gaining the opportunity for happiness. Now that you've identified your faulty reasoning, be on your guard for it. It'll never help you be a happy human. Make a note here of a time you used faulty reasoning, for example, you told yourself that it was your parents' fault you were unhappy:

Beware of the 'power pedestal': Take your parents off the power pedestal! You may be surprised by my saying that even if you blame your parents for your lack of happiness now, you're putting them on a power pedestal. By doing that you're giving them the power to control your life. So in essence you're putting them on an all-powerful pedestal, even if it's for negative reasons.

Generational transfer: It's important to ask yourself, 'Why did my parents "parent me" the way they did?' It's important to put the way your parents behaved towards you, as you were growing up, into context. This may help you if you're already a parent yourself or plan to be one in the future. They could only 'parent' you as well as the skills they were taught from their own experience of *their* parents. This is called generational transfer. Each generation transfers its know-how from parent to child, across all areas of home life – from practical things like how to look after your home, to the big things like how to be a parent. If you felt they were too strict, or unfair, or even unkind, it's likely to be due to the fact that that's all they knew as a child. They took that way of treating children on board from their parents and went on to treat you – their child – that way.

Re-parent yourself: Particularly if you feel you experienced a great deal of unhappiness in childhood, and that profoundly affects you now, you can embark on re-parenting yourself. I find people are very successful in leaving behind poor parenting and stopping the blame game when they understand the nuts and bolts of how their parents treated them. Write down here some of the things your parents did that you believe affect you now. For example, did they criticise every last thing you did? Be specific about what you write down:

The specifics: Now examine the specific behaviours you've noted about your parents and make sure you don't imitate them now in the way you treat yourself. Using the example 'My parents criticised every little thing I did', then make sure you praise every little thing you do! Emotionally speaking, you literally give yourself the emotional 'hugs' that your parents didn't give you and talk to yourself in the way that your parents didn't.

Resist becoming your parent: Sometimes we can be pleasantly surprised when we realise we're doing something or saying something just like our parents would. That happens when we have a good relationship with our parents. However this can be an unpleasant experience when we feel that we don't want to emulate them. If you have a difficult relationship with your parents, probably based in the past and the way you were parented, actively resist this when it occurs. This will help you define yourself as entirely separate from your parents in an ongoing way.

Past positives in the present: It's definitely not helpful to focus entirely on the things you think your parents did wrong.
♦ Yes, you want to separate yourself from any less-than-good behaviour on their part.

♦ Yes, you want to learn to take responsibility for your life and happiness.

♦ Yes, you want to put their behaviour in context.

♦ Yes, you want to escape the emotional echoes from the past that cause you unhappiness.

But it's important for your relationship with them, and for your well-being, to see the positives from their parenting too. Take a moment to note down some of their good intentions or things they did for you, particularly if they link in to your present life. It could be that either they link positively to the present by bringing a warm memory to mind and a smile to your lips, or they had a direct impact on, say, a positive choice you made:

Gently does it

You may have a very good relationship with your parents now and that's an excellent thing. Or when thinking about the points above you may have recognised certain behaviours in yourself that you want to change. You may also understand your parents better now even if you've had a good relationship with them as a child. Hopefully these realisations mean you're experiencing levels of happiness that aren't held back by the blame game.

Reach out

The time may be right now to reach out to your parents if your relationship has suffered in any way. The brave and courageous make the first move. You can be a brave and courageous human.

If you have difficulties with your parents *now* I'd like you to keep in mind all that I've said above about how your parents can shape your life. Also keep in mind Happiness Principle One and how it's up to you not to play the blame game.

And I'd like you to understand that it's important, even if your parents had difficulty giving you the love and warmth you wanted, that unless they were unforgivably abusive (and believe me there are some parents who should *never* be forgiven), you should show them some care and forgiveness. On the whole they probably tried to do their best by you and they've probably beaten themselves up for mistakes they've made. You shouldn't set out to 'punish' them knowing they may have got it wrong but were probably trying incredibly hard to get things right. Trying to punish your parents – or anyone else who is meaningful to you – in this way will diminish your happiness, as well as theirs of course.

As the parenting you've received is important to your well-being and happiness, so too are you and whether or not you like yourself enough to enjoy happiness. Let's turn to this now and explore your levels of self-like – and even self-love.

Build Your Happiness Habit

Each day give yourself an 'emotional embrace' that represents the best side of the parenting you've received plus your own grown-up, loving and responsible self looking after the very important You.

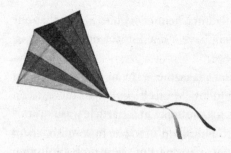

2

Dare to Love Yourself...
and Be Happier

Happiness depends upon ourselves.
Aristotle

You may never have considered what, in actual fact, is a fundamental truth behind human unhappiness and happiness, and that is *this* question: Do you actually like yourself? Do you even love yourself?

Most of us rush, plod or sail through life not considering this important principle. No matter what our levels of happiness or unhappiness are, we don't consider how it relates to our feelings about ourselves. How can this be? How can we neglect something so utterly important to happiness as the way we feel about ourselves? I'll tell you why: it's actually *easy* to neglect something this important because it just doesn't register in our conscious life.

We often aren't emotionally intelligent enough to realise that our feelings about ourselves will have a real impact right across our lives – and on our happiness.

Yes, pick up any popular magazine and you can read articles about topics like 'learning to love yourself', but often there isn't a clear link to happiness. Or the messages in the article wash over us and we fail to relate them in a meaningful way to how we feel. And of course many of us are guilty of turning our nose up at the notion of self-like. We think it sounds a bit too self-indulgent. Believe me, it's not.

The others that you like

Think about someone you like. Bring an image of them to mind. Because you like them you're prepared to listen to them. You're happy to be in their company. You're always there for them if they're down or have a problem. You do all sorts of good things for them – and with them – just because you like them. You want them to be happy and you hope you're part of their happiness.

Let's call this 'other-like' since they are literally an 'other' person that you 'like'. And when you have 'other-like' for someone you do all those positive things I've mentioned, because you're willing to be there, support them, share time with them, wish them to be happy, and so on. Those positive things symbolise that you value them and hold them in high esteem. And so what about the wonderful you – and liking you? Now that you can see the benefits of liking someone, shouldn't this apply to you, as in 'self-like'? Yes, of course it should.

Critical self-like indicators

I'd like to stimulate some immediate self-analysis and have you take a moment to consider these three critical indicators of self-like. How do they apply to you and your feelings about yourself?

Place a tick by any that apply to you:

- ☐ Are you happy to spend time in your own company?
- ☐ Do you generally feel that you're an 'all right', likeable, good person?
- ☐ Do you pat yourself on the back when you've done something well, or faced a challenge, or simply for being the good person that you are?

I hope you have ticked at least one, but maybe you haven't. Perhaps you're not even sure if you ever feel such things about yourself, like being 'happy to spend time in your own company'. Or if you ever do something like 'pat yourself on the back'. That's because they simply don't register in your consciousness. I'd like you to become more conscious of the way you feel about yourself. Then you'll be able to embrace the second Happiness Principle to come later in the chapter.

Why don't we give much time or thought to our feelings towards ourselves?

I strongly believe it boils down to emotional intelligence – or lack of it. We're not emotionally intelligent about the way we feel about ourselves because from birth to adulthood our thoughts and feelings are so wrapped up elsewhere. It's the rare parent (yes, back to those pesky parents again) that encourages their child to think about liking himself or herself. Just think of the things that get in the way of this: there are the practicalities of everyday life in a household (washing, cooking, tidying, DIY, paying bills, and so on); there is the time spent trying to get siblings to show some semblance of respect for each other; there is school work, other activities, and all sorts of distractions. Little wonder parents have no time or thought to spare to encourage children to like themselves.

Time marches on and we go to college or work, and again there are so many things that get in the way of taking the time to even consider liking yourself. Even in heartfelt discussions with friends and partners, where you talk about your life and feelings about things, it's rare that you'd actually discuss the most critical person in your life – you – and your feelings about yourself. This all too easily slips under our emotional radar.

Too much me, me, me

I'm not saying that you should become an utterly selfish person who is completely focused on yourself, spending your whole life thinking *only* about 'me, me, me'. There's a vast difference between that type of selfishness that some suffer from, and liking yourself. It's not selfish to nurture an underlying strand to your life that protects you wherever you go, and that is all about liking yourself.

How does self-like relate to happiness?

It's quite simple in principle: self-like relates to happiness because it means you appreciate and value yourself, meaning you'll look after yourself. As you'd treat another person that you like in positive ways, when you appreciate and value yourself you're much more likely to act in ways that are positive for you. In turn this means you're far more likely to bring happiness into your life. You allow yourself more happy moments and enjoy feeling happy, and you spend less time emotionally 'beating yourself up'.

But we humans tend to meander along this road of life and pay only lip-service to trying to like ourselves. Many of us find there are stumbling blocks to developing self-like and to putting into action the behaviours that confirm this. Often these stumbling blocks revolve around doubting ourselves, or not accepting ourselves, or we even fear that we'll spin into that 'me, me, me' type of selfishness

– that we'll become too self-indulgent. I'd like to reassure you with a simple truth: those who are concerned about being selfish – and don't want to be – are the least likely to be selfish.

Write down here one thing you like about yourself:

✎ ....

Write down here one thing you've done for yourself lately that's been positive or kind to yourself:

✎ ....

Self-acceptance

An important part of liking yourself is to accept yourself. Accepting yourself is a type of 'warts and all' scenario. This is because the main part of accepting yourself means accepting all your foibles and quirks, recognising your bad habits, and changing those things that matter about yourself and that you know you can improve, rather than beating yourself up over shallow things like wanting to be the perfect weight or having the perfect look. Knowing the difference between such things is one big step towards accepting yourself.

It's important to understand that those who accept themselves are able to see through many of the unrealistic myths and pressures in society. These myths and pressures damage the potential for happiness. For example, there's an enormous pressure on women in particular, but also increasingly on men, to be 'perfect'. They have to be the right size and shape; they have to have the right hair in perfect condition, and it must be dyed the right colour; their complexion has to be glowing, their make-up perfect, and their clothes in style. It's an endless list.

Then there are other myths, such as trying to be Superwoman or Superman and juggle a demanding career, an active social life, a perfect domestic life, being a great parent, being a loving partner, and so on. And while doing all of these things you feel you should maintain a wonderful equilibrium where you never snap at anyone or feel stressed or put upon.

As if anyone can live up to those ideals! But people try to, and they fail to accept less than those ridiculous aims from themselves. And so they never accept themselves, as *no one* can do all those things at the same time, and do them well.

Self-acceptance leads to self-esteem

When we come to accept ourselves – including accepting the things we'd like to change and only changing them for the right reasons – it enhances our self-esteem. Thinking about others again can help us understand this: someone that you like and respect, you'll hold in esteem. You see them as worthy of important things like your respect and consideration. Turn these feelings inwards towards yourself, and that is your self-esteem. Your self-esteem revolves around respecting yourself and being considerate to yourself. In fact research[5] shows that there are all sorts of good things related to self-esteem including the ability to regulate yourself – to know when to say yes or no, to know when to take a moment and pause, and when to take action. Thinking about you and your self-esteem, do you respect yourself, regulate yourself and expect consideration for yourself?

Our level of self-esteem – high or low – has so many consequences for our everyday lives. These definitely impact in different ways on our ability to enjoy happiness. Take the happiness we can get from an intimate and loving sexual relationship – that wonderful sense of being special to one person. Research has found that women with higher self-esteem enjoy a wonderful side-effect of that, which was longer-lasting sexual desire – important to a loving and happy relationship.[6]

These good things are part of an upward cycle that grows more positive as things like your self-respect, your understanding of yourself, your self-regulation, and so on, feed into your self-esteem. The cycle builds and grows from the strength of these related strands and gives you the power to enjoy more happiness. Or the reverse can happen and you can become locked into a negative downward cycle. This is where, say, lack of self-respect picks away at your ability to regulate yourself. In turn you make poor choices, leading to damaging behaviour. And that leads you to question yourself and have less understanding of yourself, and so on. Such a downward spiral in your self-esteem definitely decreases your chance of happiness.

Self-esteem and your happiness filter

I've found from the countless people I have worked with or met that good self-esteem provides what I call a 'happiness filter' in the person's life. Because they feel good about themselves – yes, they *like* themselves – they have a natural filter on what they allow into their inner, emotional life. Their happiness filter is more likely to filter in positive things and filter out negative things that would impact on their well-being.

For example, their day may be going along fine but the colleague who sits next to them is having computer problems and isn't going to meet a deadline. This colleague frets, moans and groans, and generally disrupts the area around them. Those with good self-esteem – and so a well-functioning happiness filter – will lend an ear to their colleague, make suggestions, but *not* absorb their colleague's stress and negativity.

On the other hand those with lower self-esteem don't have such a happiness filter working for them and may well feel obliged to take on board some of their colleague's stress. What good does that do anyone? The person with good self-esteem and a naturally functioning happiness filter realises that that doesn't help themselves or their colleague.

Your happiness filter

Think about the last time you were in such a situation: a colleague, a friend or family member was experiencing some difficulty or stress. How did you respond? Be honest with yourself: could you 'lend an ear', but *not* feel obliged to join in with their emotionality and take their stress on board – and instead filtered it out? Or did you end up feeling as they did?

Make a note here about what happened and how you felt:

 ....

The self-love cycle

The more you like yourself, accept the person you are, challenge yourself where appropriate, and use your happiness filter, the more you will begin to *love yourself*. You will *dare* to love yourself – you'll no longer feel doubt over your worthiness. You'll feel *generous* to yourself emotionally in the way you might to someone you cherish, like a partner or a best friend. It becomes a caring, loving, self-fulfilling and positive cycle that increases and builds in strength within you.

Allowing yourself to actually love yourself can be a bit daunting, as the little doubts and negative feelings of perhaps a lifetime make you feel a bit of a fraud, or undeserving of such self-regard. I know this from the stories of others and my personal experience when, after my divorce, I felt fairly unlovable. When you don't feel positively about yourself it can take time to develop the cycle of self-love.

But that's the ideal point to challenge yourself on a daily basis – or even many times a day – when you don't feel very lovable. You take one positive step and put one foot on the bottom rung of the cycle of self-love and slowly but steadily you build positive feelings about yourself. This is very often a time when you discover you have unconscious, negative feelings that hold you back. Sometimes you've absorbed these from, say, another person or an unhappy experience, as I did from my first marriage.

Your unconscious and your feelings towards yourself

As I've mentioned, up until this point you may not have consciously thought about your feelings for yourself and particularly how they might relate to your happiness or unhappiness. But believe me, at an *unconscious* level we have all sorts of feelings about ourselves that bubble under the surface of our conscious awareness. These feelings and impulses can either drive us to behave in ways that are positive, and have good and happy outcomes for ourselves and our lives, or propel us to behave in ways that have negative outcomes and bring unhappiness to ourselves and our lives.

'Mysterious' behaviour

Have you ever done something or behaved in a way that makes you think, 'Where did that come from?' Or, 'Why did I do or say that?' Think about this for a moment. Does this ring any bells? It's more than likely that it does because all of us have these moments where we are surprised by something we've done or said. Very often we immediately move on and forget about it. Sometimes these moments cause us concern because they've had an immediate impact on, say, our relationship, because something seemed to spurt forward from our mouth that we hadn't planned to say.

Then we're more likely to mull over what might have propelled us to say or do something. Rarely, though, do we have a 'lightbulb' moment where we think 'Ah ha! That feeling has been whizzing around my unconscious and it's just revealed itself.'

That's exactly what's happening, though. Your unconscious feelings, thoughts and desires influence so much of the way you feel – and what you do. That includes the way you feel about yourself and the things you do that have an immediate impact on your well-being and happiness.

If at an unconscious level you don't feel very good about yourself – you don't really like yourself – then this will definitely influence your feelings, making you unhappy. You may not know why you 'don't feel very good'. You might wonder why you feel a bit down or disheartened. You may worry that you feel unhappy too much of the time. But you find it very hard to get to the bottom of these feelings as there's nothing you can really put your finger on. And so your unconscious life continues to affect the way you feel without you consciously recognising this.

Happiness Principle Two

Find the 'likeable' in you, as once you discover it you'll go from strength to strength.

When you like yourself, you'll make sure you bring good emotions, experiences and energy (the three Es) into your life, you'll do more of what you like doing, and you'll come to love yourself. And that means finding more happiness.

Jack's unhappy story

Imagine feeling that you're simply not a very likeable person, not much good, nothing special and maybe not deserving of happiness. That was Jack. He presents a good example of how *not* liking yourself very much affects your happiness. On the outside he's the type of man that appears to have a good life. On the inside it's a very different story.

Jack was a 39-year-old section manager in a large department store overseeing about 40 staff. He was married to a nurse, Sue, and they had two young children. So far, so good. But underneath this veneer of being a successful family man Jack was unhappy – or at least not as consistently happy as he'd expect to be. In conversations it became clear that he hadn't been a 'happy sort' of person for much of his adult life. Apart from short bursts of happiness, like when he met Sue, and they had their children, he felt fairly unhappy inside.

It wasn't that Jack was clinically depressed. He had a thorough check-up, and his GP reported it wasn't classic depression. The only thing Jack and his doctor could come up with in conversation was that it appeared Jack simply had a fairly glum and lacklustre approach to life. Yes, Jack was a family man, but much of the reason he enjoyed this role was due to Sue's natural enthusiasm for family life. Yes, he'd accomplished a great deal in his work, but that was down to sheer hard slog rather than a passion for his job.

Thankfully, Sue was very supportive, despite sometimes feeling that the general level of happiness in their household was down to her more optimistic outlook towards life. As a nurse she also agreed with the GP's belief that Jack wasn't what she'd call depressed. Apart from loving his wife and children, he just wasn't a particularly happy sort of person.

Over a relatively short time in conversation it became apparent that Jack didn't think much of himself. In fact inside he didn't really like himself. When this was explored Jack made a number of revelations. At university he'd always considered himself a creative sort of person, and envisaged a career that somehow used his creativity. A department store management position wasn't what he would have predicted as his future. Various circumstances had led him down this path, though; for example, at a pragmatic level, he'd married early and wanted to support his young family. A retail opportunity arose and he took it, feeling it was a 'good' and responsible to do so. Inside, though, he thought it would be a relatively short-lived career choice before he would change the course of his work to something more creative. As the practicalities of life grew, secretly inside Jack came to feel he wasn't dynamic enough to change course. He felt that someone like himself, who could let a creative talent slip through their fingers, wasn't deserving of anything more, anyway.

Jack also revealed a huge burden he'd secretly carried all these years that confirmed to him that he wasn't a very 'good' person. His best friend when he was at university, Tom, had committed suicide in their second year. Jack couldn't shake off his feelings of responsibility for this tragic event because he'd been Tom's best friend. Over and over he told himself that he could have done more and should have realised that Tom was deeply depressed. 'Why didn't Tom turn to me?' he'd ask himself. 'If I'd been a better person he would have,' was the conclusion he repeatedly drew.

Such harsh feelings of personal failure played alongside Jack's lack of contentment in his career and feelings that if he'd been a more dynamic person his creativity would have shone through in another direction. A cycle like this established a sense within him that he wasn't a particularly good, worthy, interesting person. And in all honesty he didn't like that – and so crucially he didn't really like himself.

Jack's happy beginning

Now armed with a better understanding of these deep-rooted feelings and with encouragement from Sue, Jack undertook a number of strategies to change the way he felt about himself.

Forgiving/accepting your past self: When you can, as Jack could, identify a critical transitional time in your life that has long since affected your levels of happiness, this strategy is very useful. Jack selected a favourite photograph of himself from his university days. He put it in a brightly coloured frame so that it gave off a sense of positivity. He then meditated on his past self while looking at his framed photo. Jack was given questions focusing on two areas from that time in his life to meditate on: first about himself as a friend and second about himself as someone about to embark on the next phase of his life.

O *As a friend to Tom*: was he a thoughtless friend? Or did he care about Tom and show it? Did he, the 20-year-old Jack, possess the knowledge to decide if someone was just 'a bit down' or actually depressed? Did he have the ability to see through it if someone like Tom was pretending to be happier than they were? Could he change the things in Tom's life that had made Tom so depressed? While mulling over such questions he was to look into his youthful face in that photo and determine whether there was anything but goodwill, camaraderie and friendship there. Jack could honestly say those good things were there, and that in his youth he couldn't have predicted what was really going on with Tom, and so he deserved to forgive himself for believing he could've been a better friend.

O *As someone embarking on the next phase of his life*: Jack also meditated on questions about himself at age 21: had he been trying to do his best having met Sue so young and with plans to marry? Were his intentions to take a career-entry job, to pay the bills, good and worthy? Could he have predicted then that as two children arrived it would be hard to take a different career path? Again, looking into his own youthful face in that photo and thinking about these questions helped him to accept the good in himself and to see what a caring and responsible person he was.

Jack was to regularly remind himself of this exercise that had led him to some self-acceptance and forgiveness.

Circle of self-like: Jack was to keep a diary for three days to get a feel for any self-like and self-dislike behaviours he demonstrated. The diary was kept with a simple system. He had blue, green and red pens to hand to mark three separate things:

O A blue mark meant 'self-like behaviour' where he noticed and marked down that he'd done something that made him feel positive about himself.

O A green mark meant a 'missed opportunity' where he could have done something positive for himself, and recognised that he hadn't.

O A red mark meant 'self-*dislike* behaviour' where he did something that made him feel bad about himself – like being overly critical about a choice he'd made at work.

After the three days he counted up his three sets of different coloured marks. Jack then drew a large circle on a sheet of paper and split it into three representative sections like three slices of a pie with a red, a green and a blue slice. These slices were representative of how many marks each colour had received. He made 20 red marks over the three days, 10 green and five blue. So his circle had a large red slice taking up almost half of the pie. The green slice took up about two-thirds of the remaining section. The blue slice took up the final third of the remaining section. As Jack discovered from laying out this colourful 'circle of self-like', he actually engaged in more negative, self-dislike type of behaviours than self-like behaviours. Seeing it as a circular 'pie chart' was a graphic depiction of how he needed to increase his self-like behaviours and decrease his self-dislike behaviours.

Reclaiming power visualisation: Part of Jack's feeling of not really liking himself had to do with a sense of powerlessness. He didn't like the fact that his career marched onwards in a direction that seemed further and further away from his natural creativity. For many years he had inwardly felt useless in allowing this situation to go on. He needed to reclaim power over this important aspect of his life that was affecting his happiness. Jack was asked to visualise this sense of powerlessness with his career in some shape or form. Just doing this exercise was going to use some of his natural creativity. He decided to visualise his career, and lack of satisfaction with it, as a whirling tornado. Jack was to hold this dramatic image of the whirling tornado in his mind's eye. He was to focus on the power of the tornado and imagine himself harnessing it. This was to be his power. Jack could now 'see' through this visualisation just how much power he could harness and use positively. Next Jack was to think of at least two ways or ideas to use this harnessed power and make it work for him. The first idea he came up with was to brainstorm some creative management ideas. The idea of being more creative in the way he managed people would go at least a little way to fulfilling some of his natural creativity. The second idea he came up with was to simply appreciate the skills he used every day in his work. He'd become so hung up on criticising himself for being stuck in his career that he'd forgotten the good things he did in managing his staff well.

Jack was now feeling more optimistic about life. Sue noticed this optimism and reported that Jack seemed to enjoy more of the little pleasures in their life. Jack's optimism led him in a new direction – to visit headhunters to look at other career opportunities that might use more of his natural creativity than his present career. In the meantime he began to feel that he really did like himself and could more easily see the positive things about himself. Jack was definitely a happier human now.

How do you really feel about yourself?

Let's turn to a brief quiz that will hopefully highlight some basic truths about your feelings towards yourself. Answer each of the following questions completely honestly. Before you start the quiz I'd like to draw your attention to Chapter Five where we'll be looking at other indicators of more serious issues such as profound self-loathing and self-harming behaviours. If you treat yourself that badly, and engage in such behaviours, Chapter Five will be helpful to you.

1. Do you 'beat yourself up' very often about something you've said or done? For example, like saying to yourself, 'Why on earth did I embarrass myself like that? What an idiot!'

   A Yes, all the time
   B Yes, sometimes
   C Not at all or rarely

2. When someone compliments you how do you respond?

   A I think they've got to be joking
   B I want to believe it but I'm not sure I should
   C I appreciate it and say thanks

3. Do you ever do something nice or pleasant just for you, for no particular reason?

   A No, never
   B Rarely or occasionally
   C Fairly often

4. Do you think things like, 'I'm useless, I'm silly, I'm not much good for anything,' and so on?

   Ⓐ Yes, frequently
   Ⓑ Yes, sometimes
   Ⓒ No, I'm never that harsh about myself

5. Do you go out of your way to put others' needs, wishes or wants first, even if it's something you want or would like?

   Ⓐ Yes, frequently
   Ⓑ Yes, sometimes
   Ⓒ It depends on the circumstances – I might put my own needs first

6. Do you spend time wishing you were a 'different person' in some way (for example more likeable, more relaxed, more happy)?

   Ⓐ Yes, frequently
   Ⓑ Yes, sometimes
   Ⓒ No, it doesn't cross my mind

7. Deep down do you feel that you're not very well liked or wish you were a more 'popular' person?

   Ⓐ Yes, I feel this
   Ⓑ Sometimes I feel this
   Ⓒ No, I don't feel this

8. Would you find it fairly easy to list three good things about your personality?

   Ⓐ No, definitely not
   Ⓑ It would be quite difficult
   Ⓒ Yes, I could

Your responses

More than two 'A' answers

Too little self-like. Your answers indicate that you have little regard for yourself. This undoubtedly casts a shadow over the possibility of feeling happy much of the time. As well as looking at the strategies Jack used, try the solutions below.

More than three 'B' answers

A little self-like. As long as the rest of your answers are 'C' answers, you can undoubtedly increase your level of self-like with regular effort. Look at the strategies below and experiment with them. Discover what works for you and keep using them, especially if you had any 'A' answers.

Five or more 'C' answers

Lots of self-like. As long as the rest of your answers aren't 'A' answers, you enjoy good levels of self-like and this is marvellous! You may well experience good levels of happiness but it's valuable for each and every one of us to explore and experiment with things (like the strategies below) that may help give you consistently high levels of self-like.

Increasing your self-like

Personal exploration: It's important to try to explore why you may not have a high level of self-like. Once you know at least some of the 'why' behind your feelings, as with Jack, it becomes an easier journey towards self-like. Examine your 'A' answers. For each one think through where your impulse to select an 'A' answer comes from. Let's say, for example, you selected 'A' for question 2 – does your rejection of someone's compliment to you actually mean you don't trust what others say to you? Why else would you reject a compliment? If you have a lack of trust about others being kind to you, perhaps this links into an experience where someone broke your trust. And if someone broke your trust, can you not counter that with instances where people did as they said they'd do – and so proved their trustworthiness? Go through such exploration with each of your 'A' answers. Open your mind to why you automatically selected that answer. As in my example, ask yourself why you'd think that way to choose that answer. Personal exploration like this can be extremely valuable particularly when you can hinge your answer onto an explanation for it.

Now take a moment to consider these two questions:

Have you ever experienced a time/phase in your life where you really liked yourself? Where you had positive feelings about yourself and whatever you were doing? If you can answer yes, what was going on then? What was different about that time in your life compared to now? Make a note here:

If you can identify such a time or phase, did how much you liked yourself depend on *someone* else, say, a romantic partner, or *something* else, like a job you loved? Make a note here:

Internal versus external factors in self-like: Think about

when you've had a real sense of self-like. Did it depend on something *external* to you – like another person that makes you feel good or a job that gave you a lot of satisfaction and that you enjoyed? If so, could your self-like have been too dependent on external factors? If at that time you simply held yourself in higher regard, because you just felt pretty good about yourself, then your feelings of self-like may have depended on *internal* factors. Those internal factors are the general feelings inside you as well as the way you're thinking about things. Often people find that they have an internal ebb and flow, though, of both negative and positive emotions. And that *internal* ebb and flow of both the negative and positive is often linked to something more specifically *external*, like your boss complimenting you (giving you a positive emotion) or criticising your work (giving you a negative emotion) – but not always. So it's valuable to explore this area with an open mind, to think about whether your internal flow of feelings and thoughts tend to be quite positive, nurturing and good, or are easily tipped into the negative.

With regard to self-like, ultimately it's important to be aware of how external factors in particular influence your levels of self-like as you obviously shouldn't be basing your self-like entirely on them. Of course things like having a loving partner, or a job you love, may increase your feelings of satisfaction with yourself – and in turn increase feelings of self-like. But you can't depend on such things being in your life at all times. You need to appreciate yourself at all times regardless of external factors!

Having thought about the reasons for your 'A' answers, and external and internal influences to your self-like, here are some small steps to take for a happier beginning:

Identify your qualities: Write down your two best qualities on post-it notes and stick these in at least three places that you see regularly, such as your PC, your bathroom cabinet and your fridge. Read them each time you see them. Believe them!

A pledge to yourself: Seizing on those two best qualities and considering things such as 'other-like' – how you like other people and show it to them in positive ways – now you can make a pledge to yourself to like yourself more and behave in ways that prove this. You have the power to stick to your daily pledge. Meditate for a few moments each morning on your pledge, perhaps as you get up and start to embrace the day. If it helps to formalise it, then create your own pledge. For example it might be, 'Today I will like myself and remind myself of my good qualities.' Write your pledge here:

✎ ....

Allow yourself pleasure: Select a pleasurable activity that you enjoy but tend to put off doing because you make up excuses like a lack of time, when really you don't think it's worth bothering 'just for you'. Do bother, and make a regular date in your diary to do this pleasurable thing *just for you*.

Emotion-changing meditation: Lie back somewhere comfortable and warm, preferably in a darkened room, with your eyes closed. First allow your mind to think about something you do *not* like about yourself. Really think about the detail of it. Allow the emotion associated with it (maybe a little hurt or anger – but whatever the emotion is that you associate with it) to wash over you. *Feel that*. Now let it go and think about something you *like* about yourself. Again think about the detail of this and how it makes you feel – hopefully a bit happy. Really go with the moment and the emotion. *Absorb* that feeling and *hold* it. The next time you start to feel whatever you associate with the things you don't like about yourself, close your eyes, regain this positive feeling and try and substitute it for the negative one. Having mentioned 'anger' in this paragraph we'll be exploring the positive side to difficult emotions in Chapter Five.

Your likeableness: Write down here one thing that you've liked about yourself *today*:

✎ ....

HAPPY FACT: *The top five happiest countries all have warm climates.*

Learn to laugh at yourself!

Part of learning to like yourself – and growing to love yourself – is learning to laugh at yourself. We're all guilty at times of taking life too seriously, particularly when it comes to ourselves. Those who don't like themselves very much find it hard to lighten up and worry about things like keeping up appearances. If they make a mistake, or say something silly, they punish themselves with that negative little devil of a voice on their shoulder. Those who fret and worry through life are the least happy. Those who let go of these little things have a positive outlook and happier daily life. The next time you make a mistake, for example, challenge your punishing thoughts. Tell yourself, 'Everyone makes mistakes and my mistake doesn't matter, I can rectify it if necessary or move straight on if not'. It helps to move on by reminding yourself of this if the urge to 'beat yourself up' comes back.

We've now considered many elements in one of the most basic – and important – principles in your search to bring more happiness into your life, and that's your level of self-like. In the next chapter we're going to look at the broader horizon of your life and how claiming it *as your own* will increase your happiness.

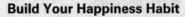

Build Your Happiness Habit

Each day look in the mirror and appraise yourself positively. Of course you can choose to look in the mirror and frown at what you see, turn away, or criticise yourself – that's easy! It's harder to look deeply and honestly at yourself, your inner self, and say, 'I like me' and 'There's so much good in me to treasure'.

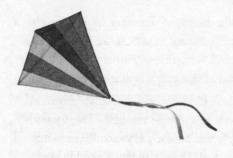

This is Your Life

*A person will be just about as happy as they
make up their minds to be.*

Abraham Lincoln

Do you ever have the feeling that you're not in charge of your
own life? That others seem to control your destiny? Or that
you're buffeted about by things beyond your control? These are
terribly important issues for many people. They feel pushed and
pulled in different directions by family, lovers, friends, colleagues
and others. They feel compelled to live up to the expectations
others have for them. They also feel pressured to fit into some
sort of social mould that dictates that you should choose to live
one type of lifestyle over another. Society tells you that you need
to be 'part of the pack' to fit in, even if for you – with your individual personality, desires and expectations – it means a poor fit.

It's easy to lose sight of yourself, and your needs, with these sorts
of pressures. They leave you feeling you're not at the helm of where

your life is headed. It's like being a passenger in a plane that's supposed to be *your* plane. You want to pilot it but find others are doing the piloting for you.

You can take control and I hope you'll find some of the themes to consider, plus solutions to put into action, in this chapter very helpful. However until you begin to believe that your life is your own – and that it won't be entirely governed by pressures from others, by social pressures, or by other forces – you won't achieve the level of happiness you could otherwise.

Chance and fate

Just as you can point to others and say they're trying to control your life, you might say and believe that chance and fate do so, too – that it's all down to 'chance' whether you end up very happy generally, or whether you enjoy periods of happiness specifically. And that it may be your 'fate' not to experience much happiness.

The findings from research into chance and fate vary, but roughly around 60 per cent of people believe in chance and fate to some degree. That is of course your prerogative, and when we come to discussing your intuition and spirituality in more depth in Chapter Eight we'll explore this more fully. However, even if you have strongly held beliefs about chance and fate, it's important to accept that you have the biggest part to play in your life. Because even if you hold dear a belief that chance and fate propel your life in certain directions you still have the choice over how *you react* to these.

External pressures – internal choices

In the last chapter I've mentioned internal and external factors, but that was in relation to your level of self-like. Here I'm thinking of the broader sweep of your life and the direction it takes. The pressure from others, and chance and fate, are two very different sources of pressure on you and your life choices. On the one hand those trying to push you in one direction (be it in something like your relationship or your career choice) are a source of *external* pressure that you can identify, that specifically comes from another person, or generally from the social group you live within. You may rightly feel such pressures are at the root of some unhappiness. But on the other hand when you give up responsibility for your life and decide your life is guided by chance and fate you also make it less likely that you'll embrace the happiness that could be yours. Again you see this as something *external* to yourself, even though you can't specifically point to any one person, but rather to a general notion of fate and chance.

Either of these can be sources of unhappiness – specific people pressurising you to do certain things or live a certain way, or believing chance and fate have dealt you a bad hand in life. But with both, it's the lack of taking charge of your life that's really the important issue.

Think 'internally'

The solution is to begin thinking 'internally' – that from *within* you comes the power (your will power!) to keep your life sailing along the course you choose. From within you arises the capability and potential to find happiness in many different ways and in different aspects of your life.

Of course it's only human at times – particularly during times of stress and unhappiness – to think others have pushed you into this or that unhappy situation, or that fate decided some unhappy event should occur in your life, and so you should feel this way. These thoughts tie in with the idea of the 'blame game' from the first chapter. Again, as with other very human feelings, it's almost easier to blame something external to yourself for your unhappiness. When you either give in to the pressures of others – and/or social pressures from the community you live in – or toss your life into the hands of fate, you give up the chance to have the satisfaction of being in control and all that means. For being in control of your life, and defining who you are and where you're going, means the following amongst so much else:

♦ creating your own happiness and enjoying happy moments
♦ reaping the rewards for your successes
♦ learning from your failures
♦ having the pleasure of looking at your available choices over a given situation and making a decision
♦ riding the ups and trying to control the downs – and so on.

Let's take a look at two things:

1 How much of your life is dictated by things that are external to you, like other people.
2 And after that, your beliefs in chance and fate.

 How much control do you take?

Answer these questions honestly and select the answer you're *most likely* to do.

1. When under pressure from others to make a different choice, or change direction on something important to you, are you likely to:

   A Stand your ground
   B Be persuaded to change your position

2. People are debating a hot topic like politics at work – will you give your point of view?

   A Yes, definitely
   B Probably not

3. Going out socially, when asked 'what do you want to do', do you say what you'd like to do?

   Ⓐ Yes, definitely
   Ⓑ No, I let others decide what we'll do

4. When faced with a big decision or dilemma, are you most likely to:

   Ⓐ Think it through and make up my mind what to do. I might ask what others would do but I'd place more importance on my feelings about it.
   Ⓑ Seek the advice of others. I'm unlikely to rely on myself to make such a decision.

5. Have you ever, or would you, confront your manager or boss if you felt overlooked for recognition or promotion? Or in similar circumstances take up such an issue with the person in charge?

   Ⓐ Yes, I would definitely discuss such a situation with them
   Ⓑ No, I'd let it go or feel unable to do so

Your responses

Three or more 'A' answers

Consistently in control and/or capable of control. This mini-quiz is simply a snapshot of your feelings in relation to being in control. With three or more 'A' answers you're likely to be aware of the importance of taking control in your life. You undoubtedly feel a desire to be in control of your life, trying to keep on top of pressures from external sources, being an individual, and so on. This is a very positive basis for increasing happiness in your life. Please look at the advice below for any 'B' answers you selected, as well as noting the other suggestions so that you can strengthen your natural inclination to take charge of your life.

Three or more 'B' answers
Lack of belief to take control. You might recognise that you're not in as much control of your life as you probably should be. There are many reasons why people give up control, particularly under pressure from others. Consider each one of your 'B' answers, in turn, in the light of my suggestions below as I work through the five quiz questions and the elements underlying them. Any 'B' answers can impact on your levels of happiness.

Taking Control

Question 1: Under pressure from others in specific situations

When under pressure from others to change something that's important to you, a starting point is to look at their motives for why they want to exert pressure on you. Why do they want you to change direction or what you're doing? What potentially is in it for them? Let's say it's your partner that wants you to increase your hours at work to help towards paying for an expensive holiday. Perhaps they already work long hours and want you to match those? Or maybe they have some personal or selfish motive for wanting you to take the lion's share of this burden? If bending to their will causes you discomfort, loss of control and any other of a host of potentially negative outcomes, then giving in will lead to at least some unhappiness. Once you've identified their motives it gives you more power to take back control of the situation.

Address these issues with clear communication. Think through what you want to say and how you can say it in the most easily understood way. Repeat the point you're making if they fail to listen to you. Finally, establish your boundaries by stating that you won't be changing your mind on this point, and that you'll only discuss it further when they're ready to acknowledge your feelings. It's very satisfying to stand your ground in a reasonable way to maintain control of something you feel strongly about.

Question 2: Your point of view

It's interesting to watch a discussion and examine the individual contributions and reactions of those involved in the discussion. When someone feels unable to give their opinion, or express a point of view, they often withdraw and simply watch others with a wistful expression. Someone who feels unable to express their point of view more often than not also feels envy of those who do. They think quietly to themselves: 'I'd love to say what I think but I just can't.' Usually they feel this way for one of two main reasons, either:

♦ that no one will be interested in what they have to say, or
♦ they may risk falling out of favour if their view doesn't tally with that of others.

Either way they don't have faith in themselves to think that their opinion is valid and worthy. How does this fit in with taking charge of your life? Because to take charge of your life you need to express to others what that means – who you are and what you're about. And one small way you begin is with a point of view – *your* point of view!

Try expressing your point of view to your nearest and dearest in the first instance. You can practise with someone you feel comfortable with to gain confidence. Always begin expressing your point of view with an 'I statement'. For example, '*I loved* that new film directed by...', or, '*I don't* think the Prime Minister should have made the decision to...'

Challenge irrational feelings that your point of view is not as important as anyone else's. Ask yourself why that should be so? Why is their point of view more important than yours? Of course you might come across someone who thinks their point is the only point – and no one else's matters – but that selfish attitude shouldn't stop you! Make a note here of a point of view you wished you'd expressed recently:

 ....

Now resolve to express your viewpoint in future, be prepared to do so, and do it with clear communication, with 'I statements'.

Question 3: Expressing a wish, desire or want

Part of the fun of being with others is the wide variety of things people might want to do. You should be part of that too. As with your point of view, your desire to do something, or wish to try something, is every bit as valid as the wishes of others. Feeling unable to say what you'd like to do, and acquiescing to someone else's suggestion, is a classic indicator that you don't feel in control of your life. If you did feel in control you'd dare to express your wishes. You'd know what you want to do with your spare time. In fact you'd have the belief in yourself that your suggestion might appeal most to others. If people are including you in plans then they should be including your wishes over what to do. Remind yourself of this when about to say, 'I'm happy to do whatever you want to do.'

Rehearsal can help – when you know you might be in a situation where others ask what you want to do, rehearse what you might say. By preparing in this way you come across confidently and are much more likely to be listened to.

A great thing to remember is that in the majority of cases people will find you more interesting if you're interested in doing something! They want to hear your idea. It's only the rare person who is so selfish, and always wants to do what they want to do, who won't be interested in your suggestion. Here's something to ponder: *Do you want to spend time with such a person anyway?*

Question 4: Facing a dilemma

When facing a problem or dilemma, do you feel you have the resources to make the right decision? Or do you doubt yourself? Self-doubt at times is absolutely natural. Sometimes it's about recognising that you don't have the skills or experience to make a decision. But regular self-doubt, plus feeling that you just don't know what to do about something, reflects a lack of control of your life. It symbolises a sense that because you aren't in charge of your life you don't know what the solution to something might be.

When in a situation where you need to make a decision, or face down a problem, increase your feelings of being in control of the situation by breaking it down into manageable pieces. Often the dilemmas we face have a number of aspects to them. These can all get wrapped up together and feel overwhelming. By picking apart the different pieces you can work to find solutions to each piece of the overall problem.

Take the 'emotional sting' out of the dilemma or challenge you're facing. You can do this by acknowledging your gut reactions, which might in fact be over-emotional. Then pause and reflect before taking a course of action. Even if things are still emotionally charged, hopefully this reflection will calm them down so you regain a sense of control.

Question 5: Seeking your due

It can be a big issue to face someone like your boss and ask for recognition or financial reward that you feel you're due, even for the person who feels in charge of their life. When we do something like this we face a sort of 'emotional' test. Will this person value us enough to hear us out? Will they agree with what we have to say? Or will we face rejection and risk them dismissing us and what we're trying to improve about our lot? In light of that, many people feel they simply can't face someone who has what seems essentially to be 'power' over them. Only those who feel they can take what's thrown at them because ultimately they have control over their own response are likely to face up to such challenges. They figure they are in charge of their life, including improving it and asking for what they feel they're due. These issues have enormous implications for your happiness and well-being. They are at the heart of how you define yourself and your value, say, in a work context.

The very first step in taking charge like this is to define the outcome you want. Whether it's a pay rise, or recognition for a project you completed, or some other aspect of you being valued, you need to have clear in your mind the desired response. Then you can prepare the best possible case for yourself. Such steps sit nicely with an attitude of being in charge of your life. When you take a moment to think through such things you have far more positive outcomes than if you're worried or panicked about facing someone like a manager with a request.

Next, keep in mind the fact that 'the worst you can imagine is not actually so terribly bad'. You may fear being turned down for a rise, you may worry you'll be brushed aside rather than recognised for something you've done, but ultimately is that something you really can't face? I think not. Does your happiness ride on such things? I hope not. Again, thinking these things through can help put them in perspective so you can cope with even a negative outcome, like having your request for a pay rise refused.

Conclusions for your happiness

To summarise the points from this quiz: you'll experience more happiness if you accept that you are worthy of having a point of view, that you recognise your voice should be heard, and that you can face the people and/or issues that might seem to have control over you. Ultimately you have control over your response to them, and this knowledge will serve you well in taking control right across your life.

Fate and chance checklist

Let's now turn to one of the other potential sources of external pressure on you: your beliefs in fate and chance. Many people aren't even consciously aware that such things influence their lives, usually because it's simply part of the way they view the world, so it doesn't register in their consciousness. However, awareness of this, and identifying beliefs that influence you in subtle ways, will help you to balance such beliefs with using the power from *within you* to take control of your life.

 How much do you believe in fate and chance?

1. Do you believe that chance, destiny or fate will bring love into your life?

   A No, I'm responsible for finding love
   B There might be a little, or some, chance or fate involved in romance
   C Yes, if it's meant to be, love will come to me

2. How frequently do you consult your horoscope, psychics or palm readers?

   A Never, I don't believe in them
   B Sometimes
   C I check my horoscope every day and frequently consult psychic types

3. How far do you try to avoid, for example, walking under a ladder, or anything else you consider to be 'bad luck', *plus* doing things like carrying a good-luck charm to ward off bad luck?

   Ⓐ It wouldn't cross my mind to do these things
   Ⓑ Sometimes I might do these things
   Ⓒ I do whatever it takes to avoid bad luck and bring good luck into my life

4. Have you ever felt that a situation or circumstance that happened to you was based on fate or that it must have been due to your destiny?

   Ⓐ No, that never crosses my mind
   Ⓑ I've wondered about such things
   Ⓒ Yes, I've definitely felt that

5. Do you believe that some people are just plain lucky?

   Ⓐ No, there's almost always an explanation for 'luck'
   Ⓑ In some ways they might be
   Ⓒ I definitely believe that

Your responses

Three or more 'A' answers

Independent of chance and fate. You're a firm believer that your destiny is not in the hands of external pressures like the power of chance and fate. It's great that you believe you control your own life and feel independent of such external influences. In terms of your well-being you need to decide how any 'B' or 'C' answers that you chose may be balanced with your basic feeling that your actions determine what happens in your life and your levels of happiness. Explore the advice below for those choosing more 'B' and 'C' answers and think how it might apply to you, potentially influencing your happiness.

If you've chosen all 'A' answers and are a true sceptic when it comes to fate, chance and destiny, then it's important to be tactful around those who may not share such strong feelings as you do. You may believe strongly in your own strength and power to help you make choices, face situations and increase your happiness, but don't ridicule others just because they don't.

Finally, your answers show that you don't believe in such external forces as chance and fate so you're likely to believe in your own power to control your life. However, be wary if you've given answers on the previous quiz about 'control of your life' that demonstrate you feel external pressures from other people, or that you yourself don't have the courage to take control of aspects of your life.

Three or more 'B' answers
Semi-dependent on chance and fate. Part of you believes that there's more to life than what we can actually see – that something like chance or fate plays a part in where our life goes and how happy we are. But this is partly balanced by a slightly sceptical side where you don't allow beliefs in an 'external force' to completely take over your life. Your open-minded attitude can be extremely positive and may mean that you're likely to consider all angles to the situations and dilemmas you face. It suggests that you're interested in what might exist beyond ourselves and our physical world, but at the same time want to feel that you control at least some things in your life.

Explore the suggestions and advice below to optimise your open-mindedness and ensure you use your inner strength to take on life and enhance your happiness.

Three or more 'C' answers
Dependent on chance and fate. Your answers suggest you may be very dominated by beliefs in external powers that 'rule' our lives. That's fine to a point and certainly in *Happy Human* I'm not judging such beliefs. However if you really believe that your own actions don't make any difference, or only a little difference, to your life – and to your levels of happiness – I can assure you that they do!

You might decide to continue seeking the advice of people like psychics, and reading your horoscope, but it's important that you weigh up the information you receive with your own feelings and thoughts about a situation. Don't blindly let others, like psychics, tell you what to do.

Think through the following suggestions

Chance and fate can be a crutch: If you're using your beliefs in fate and chance like a crutch – to stop you from having to make your own decisions – then it's time to start taking charge of your life. For example, you could continue to read your horoscope every day but then don't let it completely dominate your life and choices. Some might argue with you about your beliefs and your choice, say, to visit someone like a psychic, seeing that as ignorant. Listen to what they have to say rather than blindly accepting all the things you do.

Test your belief systems: Why not test something you believe and that, to some extent, you allow to control your life. You can leave your lucky charm at home occasionally or skip reading your horoscope. Next, be open-minded about what could happen – good things may happen without you relying on things like a lucky charm, simply because, say, your smile lights up the room when you walk into your office and people respond well to you. Such good things are about you and not because you're carrying a lucky charm, or because your horoscope said it was going to be a good day at work for you.

Challenge your beliefs with your past experience: Think about times you were unhappy, or that you had bad luck, and things didn't go your way. Where was the power of your lucky charm or your horoscope prediction then? How can they be so powerful and dominate your life when they let you down? Regularly challenge your belief system in this way.

Let go and take control: You don't have to be frightened about letting go of some of your beliefs. If, as I just suggested, you've challenged your past experience, then this should give you the courage to develop more belief in your will and strength to achieve what you want. You don't have to rely on your belief system to develop a happier life.

Accept control of your life: I'd like you to visualise yourself in control of your life. Visualisations can be very helpful in focusing your mind and delving into the natural creativity that all humans have. And with your very own visualisation you can create an image that's meaningful to you. Close your eyes for a moment and think of yourself as in charge of your life – what image comes to mind? Are you like a sea captain or an airline pilot? Are you a supremely confident person, sitting on a throne? Is your body language powerful in your image? When you feel pressure from others, capture this vision for a moment and feel your own potential power.

Why some people relinquish control to external pressures and beliefs

To develop more belief in your own power to control your life, a little understanding of why you might believe in external powers that control you, or why you bend to external pressures, can help. In the many people I've spoken to I find there tend to be three main reasons underlying such beliefs:

Upbringing: Sometimes we inherit such belief systems from our parents, who chose to believe that fate and chance dictated their life and unhappiness or happiness. That can be a very powerful influence on how you feel as an adult about such things. It's hard to shake belief systems that have been there since your childhood. This is also why other belief systems that our parents followed or believed in – like their politics or religion – are often held to be true by us as adults, even if we might rebel over these during adolescence.

Life events: A particular event or time in our life can sometimes take on a much more powerful meaning and become an ongoing influence. Let's say you were in a car accident and survived, despite a doctor at the hospital saying, 'My gosh, you had a lucky escape!' In your vulnerable state when you were shocked and in pain, injured and facing a recovery period, that thought sticks in your psyche. It's like an emotional beacon that shines there before you, giving you the message that somehow you were lucky, that fate was looking after you – and so it must be real.

Your levels of confidence: If you lack confidence for whatever reason, then you are much more prone to bending to external pressures from others and believing that fate and chance have more power over your life than they do. Sometimes it can be quite comforting, in an erroneous way, to think that others can sort out your life, or that they can help control it so that if it all goes wrong then it wasn't your fault. But that's a false sense of comfort. At other times a lack of confidence means you simply can't stand up to others when you'd actually like to. And you feel that having an external power that might guide your life, like chance and fate, will actually win out over other sources of pressure. The theme of your confidence and how it affects your happiness will be developed more fully in Chapter Six, where grabbing hold of change in your life, making and taking opportunities and seizing the moment will be discussed.

HAPPY FACT: *Endorphins are neurotransmitters that give us a sense of well-being and make us feel happy. Kick-start them with some physical activity like a brisk walk, a dance class, or even having some sex!.*

This is IT – you're not in a rehearsal!

I urge you to seriously consider this next theme. This completely ties in with the important issue of being in charge of your own destiny. The theme is: *you only have one life to live and so you should definitely live it as you see fit*. One precious life – that's all you're given. And yet we can be so foolish and run around thinking that we have all the chances in the world to do things again, to get things right, to tell people how we feel, to be happy.

This theme has come up regularly in conversations I've had with those older and wiser than I am. We can learn from our elders! I've had the privilege of speaking to many people from a generation or two before me, including my late parents. I've always made it a point to ask for their wisdom about life and what they hold dear as they approach the winter of their own lives. It almost always emerges, with their age and wisdom, that they realise an important fact which we should recognise *now*. That fact is, that this one life you have is very short and flies by. This is all you get. You don't get a repeat performance. You don't get to do something again once the moment has passed. You only have this one chance to make your life into something that is some semblance of what you'd like it to be.

Within this truth, that life isn't a rehearsal, but it's the real-deal, actually on-stage *now*, once-only shot at things, lies your potential to enjoy happiness. Invariably in conversations with these wise people, they've made the link between those who treat life with the respect it deserves – because it can't be rehearsed again and again – and those who experience a good deal of happiness. The two go hand in hand. Our elders realise you only have *now* to find, create and enhance happiness.

Recognising this gives us a head start. These conversations have given me both a profound sense of grounding and a little bit of panic, too, if truth be told. They have given me a sense of grounding, because we all need to hear this in order to start believing it *now*. And we need to hear it from people who have lived long lives, so they know what they're talking about. The thought has also given me a little bit of panic because suddenly time seems so short and you want to take charge and squeeze every bit of happiness out of life that you can. Can this be done? Yes, through embracing the Happiness Principles.

Happiness Principle Three

Take control of your life and you give yourself every opportunity to find what makes you happy.

When you feel in charge it can be exhilarating and daunting in equal measure. But when you decide you'll attempt to control or face what daunts you, you can take your life in the direction you wish. Along the way it can at times be an exciting journey and in facing life this way you'll enjoy many rewards.

Charlotte's unhappy story

We all want to be encouraged in our dreams and passions. Secretly inside we all have wishes, desires and dreams and when we let people in to them, we hope for their support. We want them to encourage us because being able to fulfil our dreams will bring such happiness.

That's exactly what Charlotte longed for. Charlotte, 26, works in the music industry as PA to the head of a busy marketing department. Charlotte had always wanted to be a singer-songwriter, but at the time I met her, she was very demoralised. Although she had the drive and desire to pursue her dream, she'd never received much encouragement from those around her, especially in recent years. In fact the situation was quite the opposite over the last couple of years as her fiancé and family constantly reminded her 'how hard it was to make it in the music industry' and pressured her to think about taking her life in other directions.

Charlotte of course realised it was hard to make it in music but explained how disheartened she felt that no one seemed to have any faith in her. She would have liked some positive support even if people felt it was an extreme, uphill battle. Two years ago when this job opportunity arose she was pressured by her fiancé, Steve, to take it for financial security. He kept telling her how 'at least it was a job in the right industry', and as he reminded her, 'It's a million to one you'll ever make it as a singer-songwriter.' Steve wanted them to buy a flat, rather than rent, so he was keen that she brought in as much money as he did. Before taking this demanding, full-time position she'd been working as a waitress so it was easy to take opportunities for gigs when they came up. She could swap shifts with another waitress and go and play the music she loved. That's what made her really happy! Now, though, her hours were so long and inflexible that she hardly had time to practise, let alone consider playing a gig.

But Charlotte was also invested in her relationship with Steve, having got together five years earlier at university, which made this issue difficult: she wanted to stay with him, he wanted to stay with her, plus he also wanted to set up a proper home. Part of her felt he was probably right, yet still she felt hurt when Steve said things like, 'If you were going to make it then you probably would have done so by now.' He ignored Charlotte when she reminded him that Dido and Anastacia, for example, had both found success around the age of 30.

Charlotte's parents agreed with what they saw as Steve's 'very sensible attitude'. Although they said it would have been wonderful for Charlotte to realise her dream, they felt she really had to keep her feet on the ground. They insisted that was the only way to have financial security in the future. Charlotte confided that she felt her life 'wasn't her own'. She felt the people she loved most misunderstood her. Charlotte believed they ignored her feelings and weren't prepared to consider various lifestyle options as they were so concerned that she had security.

Charlotte confided how very unhappy she was. Her story is a classic one of how someone can be pushed down a particular path, even by the people who love them most in the world, that feels like the wrong path. And how someone comes to feel they have no control over what should be *their life*.

Charlotte's happy beginning

Cognitive control: Part of taking control of your life, particularly when you feel pressured by others, includes clarifying your own thoughts about the issue(s). It's understandable that when you have your own concerns whizzing around your mind, as well as the wishes of others closing in on you, you might feel a bit overwhelmed. That's how Charlotte felt. To stop feeling as if she was drowning in such a whirlpool of conflict she needed to regain cognitive control – that's the control of your cognitive processes, or 'thinking'. Charlotte used this practical strategy:

○ First she made a list of the different areas involved in the issues she faced. These included: her desire to try and achieve some success in music, her desire to stay with Steve, Steve's view of her potential to make it in the music world, how she felt about buying versus renting, how she was made unhappy by these pressures, what part her parents played in the pressure she felt to take a 'sensible and secure' path, and her wishes to please them. She separated these into two lists: emotion-based and practical-based issues and considerations. So her desire to make music, stay with Steve, feelings of unhappiness over the pressures, and wanting to please her parents went into the emotion-based list. Buying versus renting a place to live, having a secure job, and looking for new work that would give her more flexibility went into the practical-based list.

○ Charlotte next prioritised which of the two lists she wanted to make progress with first. It was the emotion-based list. She wanted to ensure that she and Steve were secure in their relationship. Not only was this important to her as she loves Steve very much, but she believed that if they felt more secure as a couple, she would feel more secure asserting her need to pursue music.

Clear communication: Now that Charlotte felt her mind was more settled on these matters, she wanted to ensure she communicated clearly with Steve about them. Thinking back to the '*How much control do you take?*' quiz earlier in this chapter, and the solutions for taking control when others are pressurising you, Charlotte planned how she could do this with Steve, and secondarily at some point in the near future with her parents. She considered his motives for being against her trying to pursue music – financial security and not throwing away money on rent – and thought about where these motives came from. She wanted to take the emotional sting out of what were powerful emotional issues to ensure their next conversation was successful. She practised how to express herself and how to demonstrate that she'd thought through different work and financial options that they could consider. Charlotte was well prepared by the time she sat him down for their next conversation.

Optimise your strengths: Charlotte felt that her powerful desire to give herself more time to try and 'make it' had got lost in the mix of their conflicting views about how their life should move forward. She was determined to express this to Steve clearly and in a way that optimised her strengths. She did this by looking at more flexible work options and their financial implications, and finding out about acoustic sessions she could play at. This demonstrated maturity and planning – that she wasn't just doing things on a whim – and showed her strengths when it came to trying to carry through her dreams.

Over a series of discussions, Charlotte and Steve came to understand each other's feelings better. They both agreed that a good compromise was for Charlotte to go back to flexible work for the next two years to give herself a good shot at music. Going back to watch Charlotte play acoustic sessions reminded Steve how much he enjoyed watching her in their first two years together. As for Charlotte's parents, they were incredibly supportive of Charlotte and Steve's new plan. When they sat down for an honest conversation they wholeheartedly took on board what Charlotte had to say about the pressure she'd felt from them. They'd never intended to hurt her feelings about her music. They also acknowledged they'd overstepped the mark in pressurising her to think about her security. Typically of many parents, they loved their daughter very much and simply wanted the best for her, but the way they did that had impinged on Charlotte taking control of her life. One year later Charlotte doesn't have a record deal, but she's still trying, and enjoying every minute!

The future-dependent happiness trap

Thinking about the fact that *life is not a rehearsal* brings me to the future-dependent happiness trap. I'll explain this to you using myself as an example because I've previously been guilty of falling into this trap. In my first marriage I got stuck in the trap of thinking things like:

◆ I'll be happy when my husband treats me better.
◆ I'll be happy if I can just get through the next few months.
◆ I'll be happy once he sticks to his promises to behave better.

And so on, and so on. 'Happiness' for me at that time was something 'out there' in the future. It wasn't something that I felt entitled to at that actual time. How wrong could I be!

But I wasn't alone in the way I looked at happiness as some sort of 'prize' to be won in the future if certain things changed. Almost everyone I've ever met has fallen into this trap – at least until the time that their eyes were opened up to it.

Why do we fall into this future-dependent happiness trap? Because we don't actually believe we have the power to change our life today, now. Because we get wrapped up in some sort of pressure, situation, issue, and so on, without seeing three things about it: that one unhappy or difficult situation shouldn't dominate our whole life; that we can embrace happiness and bring it into our life now, even in small ways, when we're facing a big issue; and finally, if the issue is that big and casting an unhappy shadow over our life, we should darned well do something about it. *Open your eyes to this now.*

Do you ever say, feel, or think:

- I'll be happy once I pay off my car, my mortgage and so on.
- I'll be happy once I find a partner.
- I'll be happy once I divorce this person (as I thought).
- I'll be happy once I get a new job.
- I'll be happy once I finish this training.
- I'll be happy once I have had children.
- I'll be happy once my children have grown.
- And so on!

If you can say, 'Yes, I have thought or felt that way,' or you do so now, then you've fallen into the future-dependent happiness trap. This trap prevents you from taking control of your life *now* because you're likely to resign yourself to happiness being 'out there' in some abstract future.

Focus your mind with these little strategies
Make a brief note of a moment when you felt happy today. It doesn't matter what inspired it or if it was brief or a nice, long extended feeling of happiness.

Today I felt happy when:

✎ ....

Describe what it is that stops you from being happy now, and how you feel you will be happy when it's changed (as in my example when I used to say and believe I'd be happy when my first marriage changed).

When I think about being happy in the future it's because of:

✎ ....

Write an affirmation about why you deserve *not* to be future-dependent for happiness – for example, 'I deserve happiness now and shouldn't have to wait for anything in my future!' Or, 'Life is short and I want to feel or find happiness now!'

✎ ....

Is the thing that holds you back from happiness now – or that needs to be changed in order for you to stop thinking that your happiness will only come in the future – something *internal*, within you (say, having low self-esteem), or *external*, something about another person who affects you and your happiness, or due to something like your job?

I'll have future happiness when I change something about (for example, 'myself and my low self-esteem')

✎ ....

What steps can you take to give you control over this?

I can take the following steps:

✎ ....

Resolve to take control of your future-dependent beliefs and reaffirm what you can do about them now.

Regrets . . . I've had a few

As well as those who look at happiness as something that will come to them in the future, I find there are those who get stuck in the past and have many regrets. They also tend to live life as if it is a rehearsal. They get bogged down in the past and spend far too much time regretting things they should have done, or they shouldn't have done, or they wish they'd done, and so on.

You might think everyone has regrets, and so what? To some extent you'd be right that of course everyone has regrets – because we're only human we sometimes do regrettable things – but if you're plagued by these regrets then it will cause you unhappiness.

Regret can actually be good. Yes, regret can serve a worthy purpose. That purpose is not to repeat the things that have caused you regret, or to become stuck in that regret and wish you could do things all over again. So with any regrets you have, you need to examine what you can do to make amends, and/or put them behind you, and then move on.

But many of us don't do that. We don't act on the things we've done, that are regrettable, to put them right. Or we don't accept that they are best left behind and forgotten because nothing can be done about them.

How much regret imposes itself on your life?

It's good to take a moment to think about your regrets. Write down here something that lingers in your mind that you feel regret about:

✐ ....

As in the paragraphs above about future-dependent issues, make a note here if there's something you can do to lay your regret-ghosts to rest:

✐ ....

Forgiveness

I mentioned forgiveness in Chapter One in relation to your parents. Now it's time to forgive yourself your regrets, accept that where you can you'll make amends, and where you can't you'll move on.

The way we define ourselves

An important aspect of being in charge and control of our lives is how we define ourselves. This is because the more we understand and define ourselves and all that goes with that understanding – such as being aware of our needs for love, connection, achievement, and so on – gives us a sense of control over our life. And, for example, how to live life so that we fulfil our needs. This has many implications for how happy we are. For example, one survey of 20-somethings found that concern over the direction their life was taking, who 'they were', and what they should do, made many of them very unhappy.[7] Their happiness was very dependent on how they saw themselves. And that is true for all age groups.

We give little conscious thought to who we are. It's often someone saying something to us about what we're 'like' that pricks a bit of self-awareness. So a partner tells us we're 'too dependent', or a colleague says we're 'too conscientious', or a friend says that we're 'a killjoy' because we want to stay in on a Saturday night. Then inside we might think, 'Am I really too dependent, too conscientious, not much fun?'

We should pay attention to what others say about us because of the dynamic interaction we have with others. We influence them, and they influence us, and it's an ongoing cycle in relationships. Part of our definition of ourselves is how people respond to us – and they respond to us because of *who they think we are* and *what they think we're like*.

The way we respond to someone else telling us they think we have such-and-such personality traits depends on our relationship with them. How much their view affects us is usually bound up with how much we care about them (like a partner or friend) as well as how much their actions affect our lives (like a colleague). When a partner tells us that we have a certain aspect to our personality, or that we're made a certain way, it means a great deal to us. We share our life with them, after all. We want them to like the person we are!

But that's not the whole picture. Again it comes back to being in charge of our life, and defining who we are, from our own perspective.

So who are you?

There are many potential ways, or 'models' as psychologists call them, of defining who we are. Some might try to define us as a set of personality traits from which spring predictable behaviour patterns. Others try to define us as having an essential 'spirit' to our character. Others might define who we are purely on the basis of our behaviour, ignoring all that goes on behind it. One thing's certain, as with so many of the things that are important to our happiness, who we 'are' is a dynamic process: who we are now is different in some ways to who we were a year ago and how we'd define ourselves in a year from now. And I believe in some ways who we are can never be truly defined because we are greater than the sum of our personality traits, attitudes, thoughts and feelings, plus the way we behave, put together.

In fact you might question why we should even think about it. But I'd say that's defeatist. A little self-reflection can be very important in learning to understand why you feel, think and act in certain ways. With that in mind, in *Happy Human* I think it helps to define who you are by looking at three broad themes:

1. Our very human needs, like the need to feel loved and to love, the need for emotional connection to others, to feel part of a

group, and so on. These define us in profound ways; for instance, are you the sort of person who flourishes when you can love another? Or do you flourish when you have a lot of independence from others? And this aspect of ourselves determines to a large extent the relationships we have, and our well-being.

2. Our most basic personality traits, which provide a constant thread throughout our life, like whether we're outgoing or a natural listener, whether we're a 'planner' or spontaneous, whether we're studious and serious or silly and fun-loving, and so on. This aspect of who we are has implications for relationships and also life choices, such as the career we choose to do.

3. Our smaller but still important quirks, foibles, tastes, likes and dislikes. These really establish us as individuals and have implications for our relationships (again!) as well as things like how we spend our spare time – our leisure time, hobbies, and so on – and what we do within our own homes, for example spending time cooking up a storm or stocking up on ready meals, keeping our home tidy or not, decorating, and so on.

Taking those three strands, give an example of each that defines who you are:

1. My human needs (for example, I need/don't need love in my life):

✎ ....

2. My broad personality traits (for example, I'm 'outgoing'):

✎ ....

3. My quirks, tastes, likes (for example, I enjoy experimenting with home decorating):

✎ ....

Cherish your uniqueness

It's important to cherish who you are – your unique self. That's because your unique self is what makes *your* life what it is. I find from the experience of working with literally thousands of people over the years that once you begin to recognise some of what defines you, you tend to appreciate yourself more. This becomes a positive, upward cycle of recognising your worth, valuing yourself, and that in turn helps to ensure that you expect others to value you, too.

Put this into action at appropriate times. Highlight your qualities when, say, a colleague asks for someone with a particular quality to volunteer for a project. Or when someone like a brother or sister says, 'Oh, you *always* behave that way!', let them know you're not so entirely predictable and that you might have spontaneous reactions different from your previous reactions. Challenge the person who puts you down and let them know you won't tolerate such treatment. Your belief in yourself and who you are will stand you in good stead for standing up for yourself. You're important. Cherish yourself, and that will give you increased levels of happiness.

Don't develop Sheep Syndrome!

When you don't believe in yourself and your ability to take charge of your life, when perhaps you don't really *understand* yourself and your needs, it's easy to develop Sheep Syndrome. This is where you simply follow the group or an individual, like friends or a partner. Sheep Syndrome can sweep across your life, for example in bending to family pressure to choose a particular profession. Your life becomes dominated by this choice that wouldn't have been yours – but you went along with it.

Leaning towards Sheep Syndrome can make smaller ripples in your life. For instance, going along on a holiday suggested by your partner to a place that didn't interest you; surprise, surprise, you don't have a very good time. But, hey, you're a sheep, aren't you?

So what did you expect? It's time to do something about it if this is the way you've been living.

To be honest we're all guilty of a bit of Sheep Syndrome on occasion, say, because we're tired, or we've made some tough decisions recently and almost prefer that someone else takes charge of another decision – and we go along with it. That's absolutely fine but it's a very different thing to live your life that way all or most of the time. It's surprising how easy it is for some people to be swept along as in a herd of sheep, giving no real thought to the consequences of their lack of decision and personal responsibility. But consequences there are. You turn around one day not feeling very happy about things and think, 'What am I doing?', and 'I didn't choose to do this!' whatever 'this' happens to be.

It's easy to spot the signs of someone who's been caught up in Sheep Syndrome: they may have little zest for life, have lost their spark, may not have a lot to say, may not have an opinion of their own, go along with whatever's suggested, and don't do important things like stand up for themselves. This way of relating to the world doesn't lead to happiness.

By exercising your right to control your life you won't be caught up in Sheep Syndrome. As I mentioned earlier in this chapter, making sure you do things like giving your point of view and having your voice heard will prevent you falling into this trap. Try a quick visualisation that can be helpful in keeping yourself focused on being your own person: try visualising a herd of sheep with *your face* on one of them, in the middle of the herd, being swept along. Hardly an inspiring visualisation!

Do you like what you're doing?

Having discussed different aspects of defining yourself and your life, and having highlighted an issue like family pressure to give up your dream profession without a fight and do something that wouldn't be your choice (as in Charlotte's story), brings me to exactly that – what you do for most of your day. If you're working you spend roughly one-third of your life doing your job. Considering that, it's important at a very human level to have some job satisfaction. It's incredibly dehumanising to be stuck for hours of your precious day doing something you hate or are unhappy about for any number of reasons. In such circumstances it's feeling that lack of control in your life – spending hours and hours doing something without any satisfaction – that's so frustrating and demoralising. In fact research shows that those who feel the most control in their workplace are the happiest workers.[8]

At the very least, if you're unhappy in your work, then taking control and exploring extra training to gain new skills, and researching other options, can help you take back a sense of control. Unfortunately you may well believe you're stuck with your job even if you hate it. Research shows such beliefs are common, yet they are terribly destructive to happiness. We live in a time with good access to skills training, additional learning, and opportunities to try new things. So career-happiness needn't be an elusive dream.

Again, as with parenting, your career satisfaction is a topic worthy of an entire book, and so I don't want to go into the specifics of career happiness. However by far the majority of the ideas, themes and Happiness Principles in *Happy Human* will apply in some shape or form to improving your work life. With that in mind, here are a few simple steps to help you begin to get control of your work life:

♦ *Fantasy and fact*: First, let your mind relax and take yourself into your fantasy world. In the realms of fantasy, what job do you dream of? Is it something that maybe you *could* do as a career? Or is it something that might make a good hobby and so you'd get some real satisfaction pursuing it as such? Let's say you dream of being an actor; then taking evening classes or joining an amateur dramatics society would give you a taste of it. You have the potential to find out so much about yourself – for instance you might find you're not good at acting, but you love making the scenery or assisting the director. Explore your fantasies and you might find out some facts about hidden talents and opportunities that can help them become a reality.

♦ *Skills training*: Next, look at any skills training your company might offer. You might end up finding job satisfaction and increased happiness staying in your company but *doing something else*. Most managers are more than happy for employees to develop additional skills. A new skill may just give you the edge in your job that makes it satisfying to you.

♦ *Job swapping*: Arrange a job swap in your company. Your company might already do this or may be happy for you to suggest it. An in-house job swap usually occurs over a single day or a week. This is where you and another colleague agree to swap jobs for a limited time, and it gives you the chance to 'live in someone else's shoes' for the day. Even if you decide their job isn't for you it'll give you more respect for what your colleague does.

♦ *Volunteering*: It's definitely worth trying volunteering for the occasional day in an industry that interests you. Even if you're landed with the more mundane jobs you can still get a feel for what others are doing. It's great for your CV, too, to have shown an interest in a variety of companies.

♦ *Improve your lot*: Finally, if circumstances prevent you moving on from your present job, then definitely discuss with your manager how to improve your situation. There may be things you can do to make it more interesting, to give you more responsibility, to ease any stresses and strains, and so on.

These small steps are the beginnings of taking charge of the many hours you spend at work. When it comes to improving your work situation it's definitely true that it's nothing ventured, nothing gained – so get going and explore your options, starting today. The hours you give to your work are crucial to your happiness – make the most of them.

We've explored a number of themes that involve you taking charge of your life. I'd now like to look more closely at two different, but important, types of happiness – and how understanding these will help you find more.

> **Build Your Happiness Habit:**
> Express a point of view each day – even over something small – and start building your self-knowledge and self-belief.

4

Bigger Picture, Smaller Picture Happiness

Happiness is as a butterfly which, when pursued, is always beyond our grasp, but which if you will sit down quietly, may alight upon you.

Nathaniel Hawthorne

I said in the introduction that I didn't want to get bogged down with a definition of what happiness is or isn't, because we experience happiness and well-being in such personal and unique ways that specifically trying to define it, and establishing a 'benchmark of happiness' that you'd hope to attain, doesn't really make sense. What's important is that you understand yourself and your life enough to know what makes you happy – and what you might be doing that makes you unhappy, often without even realising it.

One aspect of this great, big, beautiful world of happiness that I do think is helpful to clarify is what I call **Bigger Picture Happiness** (BPH) and **Smaller Picture Happiness** (SPH). Exploring these two themes can help you break down parts of your life so that you can understand them better in the way they relate to your happiness or your unhappiness. That understanding enables you to take steps to improve and enhance them. What these two themes do is to help bring a little order to the complexity of our thoughts and feelings when it comes to developing and embracing more happiness.

Bigger Picture Happiness and Smaller Picture Happiness

Before I go into the detail of each, let me broadly explain BPH and SPH.

Think of BPH as like the broad strands of your life that are more constant and influence overall levels of happiness. These constants in your life don't necessarily change very quickly – although they can change. The broad strands include things like your personality traits, beliefs and attitudes, plus your important connections (or lack of connections) to others at the levels of family, friendship and romance. They also include your satisfaction at work, overall health and financial security.

SPH can be thought of as those definable and largely unique moments of happiness and joy that occur in daily life. They punctuate our life, sometimes spontaneously and when we least expect them, or they may be something that's planned, and that we expect to be a happy event, like inviting a friend over for dinner. When it comes to a moment of happiness or joy that's unplanned, it can include anything and everything that brings a smile to your face. Perhaps this is when your cat climbs into your lap and starts purring and you feel a warmth and happiness wash over you. Or it's when you find yourself standing in the supermarket checkout queue and you receive a spontaneous smile from the child in front that's shopping with its mother. SPH includes all of these momentary feelings of happiness – expected or completely unexpected.

The canvas of your life

I like to think of BPH and SPH as the range of strokes an artist has when painting a picture on a blank canvas. Let's imagine that your life is like a canvas on which the broad and bold strokes across it – depicting the earth, the ocean and sky – are your BPH. They are the constants in your life that form the backdrop across the painting. These constants that sweep across the canvas are your personality, your connections (or lack of) to others, your contentment (or lack of it) in your career, and your health.

Then you have the detailed strokes of the smaller things that are going on in the painting – these are your SPH. These more delicate and defined strokes, which form the intricacies of the painting, represent the smaller moments of joy and glimmers of hope scattered across your life. Together they form one big canvas of the potential your life has for happiness.

How do you feel about the canvas of your life? Is it a big, bold, picture of happiness? Or are there dark clouds scattered across it? Or even violent storms? Hold your image for a moment. I think it's terribly important to tap into the creative side of your mind when thinking about your overall happiness and trying to envisage what you'd like your life to be like. Perhaps it's only a few scattered, lighter brushstrokes that would brighten up your canvas. Or maybe it would take bolder brushstrokes to rid it of any dark clouds and bring it to life in a happier way. Visualise your altered canvas *now* with the changes you'd make to it in progress. I don't say 'completed' because of the dynamic nature of our lives, and all of our canvases change from time to time.

HAPPY FACT: *Britain came 108th in the international happiness stakes.*

Bigger Picture Happiness

Let's think about BPH in more detail. The strands I listed that form your BPH – your personality, your relationships (family, friendship and romantic), your work satisfaction, health and financial security – are all important. These BPH strands are very similar to those cited in recent research as 'the big seven sources of long-term happiness'.[9] This research indentified the seven sources as: health, income, quality of work, family and relationships, the strength and safety of communities, and the prevalence of unselfish values.

One difference between what I'd like you to consider, and what that research considers important, is the strand in your life that I include of your *overall personality* in relation to happiness. However as I see overall personality as including your attitudes and beliefs, and that in turn includes things like the 'unselfish values' (such as fairness, respect for others, and so on) mentioned by this research, then there is definitely overlap.

One very interesting finding of this research was that three of their 'sources of long-term happiness' have *improved* since the 1950s: these are health, income and quality of work. In some ways I agree with that but in other ways I question it. Yes, we've had vast improvements in our knowledge of health and related issues, but far more people lead unhealthy lifestyles by overeating and under-exercising. I've met many people who feel out of shape and overweight and they find this distinctly impacts on their energy levels as well as their happiness. Perhaps you fret over an unhealthy lifestyle, worry about feeling out of shape and being overweight. I know how such worries can drag a person down on a day-to-day basis and eventually impact negatively across their life, because I hear from so many in that situation.

Likewise this research suggests that the quality of our workplace has improved, and again in some ways it has – for example, sexual harassment, something that was commonplace a few decades ago, is now illegal. Or if you are harassed, at least you can do something about it. But people find themselves doing increasingly long hours and are expected to multitask because of job losses. Often they have had to take over the work that others used to do, as jobs have been shed but output remains the same. You might well be in that situation. Have you found that increasing responsibilities have caused you stress about work? I wouldn't be at all surprised. Over the last five or ten years I've had many people confide in me that where they were once happy in their jobs, they now feel extremely put upon. It doesn't take a genius to work out that they're now unhappy about this very large part of their life.

This research also found that the other four sources of happiness have *diminished* since the 50s – family and relationships, the strength and safety of communities, and the prevalence of unselfish values. And that doesn't surprise me in the slightest.

All of these 'seven sources' of happiness are important to your well-being, and it's interesting that overall one part of them has apparently improved (remember the question marks I just raised over this), whereas the other part, for example relationships and the way we treat each other through unselfish values, has diminished. This is terribly important to grasp because the sources of happiness that have decreased *have more impact* on your overall happiness. I truly believe that the quality of your relationships is most important to your happiness, and this belief is confirmed by an extremely large global survey finding that relationships are more important than ever to us when it comes to our overall happiness.[10] Yet, sadly, they have been diminished in our lives.

The importance of relationships to our happiness is going to be discussed in much more detail in Chapter Six. And how the world has changed over the last few decades, and how this impacts on our happiness, is going to be discussed in detail in Chapter Ten. So now I'd like to continue with other thoughts on BPH.

Other aspects of Bigger Picture Happiness

A great part of your BPH is determined by your ability to recognise what's important to you and those around you. Throughout your life, being able to recognise what you care about, what works for you, what affects you most, and so on, helps to shape your BPH. Many people are unhappy for this very reason – they go through life never taking notice of what *really* affects them. They don't recognise when they're doing things that jeopardise their happiness, and maybe they even go through life with blinkers on as to what's really important. When they do this they fail to prioritise what's vital in their unique life.

Let's take the classic workaholic who thinks their job satisfaction is the be-all and end-all of their happiness and their life. They think that achievement will make them happy. They easily relegate relationships to second place because their great big aim is recognition and self-worth through what they do, rather than recognising that who they are – and who they relate to – is what has the potential to give them much more happiness in life. The classic workaholic is so blinkered to everything else in their life that they stop being able to *recognise* what's truly important.

But you certainly don't have to be a workaholic to fail to recognise what's important to you. You can be blinkered to life for many reasons, such as your fears (this will be explored in Chapter Seven), or addictive behaviours like excessive drinking (to be discussed in Chapter Five).

Recognise your priorities

Take a moment to make a note of the three top priorities in your life right now, and put them in order of the most important first, running down to the least important:

PRIORITY 1 ....

PRIORITY 2 ....

PRIORITY 3 ....

How have these changed in the last five years, if at all?

✎ ....

How do these affect your happiness or unhappiness now?

✎ ....

For example, if your main priority was to have a happy marriage but you divorced three years ago, you could say that not meeting this priority has caused you unhappiness in recent years.

A big balancing act

Another important aspect of BPH is how easily you find a balance between all the big strands and elements of your life. Finding this balance between these strands ties in with being able to recognise your priorities. Think of balancing the important things in your life as being like juggling: to keep the balls in the air, flowing smoothly, the juggler needs to keep them in balance. He anticipates what move to make next. He is always thinking one step ahead about what he can do to ensure he keeps that smooth flow going between the balls.

Achieving balance between the important strands and elements of your life means:

♦ A sense of harmony
♦ A sense of well-being
♦ A sense of accomplishment
♦ Good relationships with others
♦ Less stress and anxiety
♦ More happiness

How do you achieve this balance? Mainly by recognising that, like the juggler's balls, the elements of our lives are always shifting and changing, even if only slightly. When you recognise this then you open your mind to being more prepared for these changes. And much of being prepared comes down to your personality.

Balancing act action

One immediate way to start balancing your top priorities is to take the list of priorities that you noted above and write down all three of them on each Monday in your diary. Then, each Monday, make a quick note throughout the days of the week of how you can spend a little time balancing these priorities. For example, make a note to ring your best friend on Tuesday for a catch-up call. And book in some special time for your husband or wife, for example, on another day.

Your personality and achieving a happy balance

The subject of personality is another vast and important area. Aren't so many of the things that relate to our happiness? There are many interesting books about personality written by researchers in this field. But in *Happy Human* I simply want to touch upon personality here and how it relates to achieving balance in your life.

Just think about you and what you consider to be your 'personality'. I'm sure if I gave you a whole page of adjectives you could select many that apply to you in some circumstances or situations, but maybe not in others. And depending on the people you're with, some may become more relevant to your personality than others. Let's take the adjective 'carefree'. You might be carefree around your best friends and even become the life and soul of the party in their company. As far as they're concerned, if asked to describe one of the key things about your personality they might say that you're 'relaxed and fun'; in other words, 'carefree'. But would your manager at work describe you that way? Maybe, if your work required you to be carefree, but probably not. Would the minister at your church describe you that way? Again, probably not, unless you were responsible for providing the fun and games for the Sunday School children, and then they might describe you as carefree.

You can see how tough it becomes to describe your personality adequately because it changes and adapts between situations, and depends on whom you're with. One personality trait may express itself more strongly in one set of circumstances, like being carefree when out with your friends, but then fade into the background in other circumstances, like in a meeting with your boss. That said, in your heart you probably feel there are essential parts (or traits) of your personality that don't change all that much regardless of the situation and the people you're with. For example, how sincere and how trustworthy you are probably remains constant, as do traits like how flexible you are.

When it comes to achieving a happy balance between the priorities of your life there are certain personality traits, like being 'flexible', that make this more easily achievable. Look at the following checklist and select the Yes or No answer that best describes you. *Remember that your complete honesty is necessary!*

Achieving a balance

1. Do you like to consider many sides to an argument/issue/problem?

    Yes   No

2. Do you consider yourself 'easy to please'?

    Yes   No

3. Do you consider yourself flexible when someone wants to change plans?

    Yes   No

4. Would you be happy to swap duties with another person when someone else has just handed out a list of duties?

    Yes   No

5. Do you like or enjoy surprises, or like to surprise others?

    Yes   No

6. Once your mind is made up about something, do you find it easy to change given the right circumstances?

    Yes   No

Your responses

Five to six 'Yes' answers

Very flexible. You're likely to consider many sides to something as well as being open-minded to changes in circumstances and situations. As long as you don't simply bend over backwards to please others, say, as in the last chapter when we considered people who won't express their point of view because they don't want to be rejected by others, then this is a very good quality. The reason for this is that it means you're likely to have the personality trait of flexibility (remember this is a brief, 'snapshot' type of quiz and not a definitive personality test). That means you're likely to juggle those balls – your priorities – in the smoothest possible way, even as circumstances change. You're flexible enough to try to keep your priorities in balance with each other, and that will help enhance your levels of happiness.

Three to four 'Yes' answers
Quite flexible. In terms of your personality and the trait of flexibility you undoubtedly find some balance in your priorities. You are able at times to see when priorities might need shifting, but at other times don't feel able to rise to such challenges. Take note of some of the advice below to help increase your levels of flexibility.

Nought to two 'Yes' answers
Inflexible. You might find it hard to juggle priorities as and when necessary. This lack of flexibility might depend on the circumstances you're in or the person you're with. However, I find that those who feel and act the least flexible, when actually the situation and context really call for flexibility, do so for two main reasons. Either they lack confidence about doing something differently, and that includes things like re-prioritising aspects of their life; or they have an absolute confidence that their way is 'the only way' and they keep on a very straight and narrow path throughout life. Neither of these is particularly conducive to enhancing your levels of happiness.

How to improve your flexibility
Test the waters: It could be very beneficial to you generally, and to your happiness specifically, to be more willing to try things out. Let's say you answered 'No' to Question 4, and you'd want to stick

to the original duties that were handed out from a list. Consider these questions: Why would that be the case? Is it because you feel there's some sort of natural order to things and they should remain that way? This type of inflexibility can seep into all areas of your thinking and relating to the world, and definitely impacts on how you prioritise your life. Instead, when you next have the opportunity to test the waters, then do so. If someone suggests, say, swapping a duty at work, discuss it with them. Don't just say 'No' automatically. From this example of the smallest level of the trait of inflexibility, which you can change and allow to become more flexible, you get positive ripples outwards into the rest of your life.

Do the reverse: If your natural inclination is always to do something in your life in one way, when it comes to your priorities try the *reverse* of that. Because at some point the reverse of what you might normally do could be a good response that would actually benefit you. For instance, let's say you prioritise your career over and above your romantic relationship as well as friendships. Your boss tends to get in touch with you every other weekend and asks if you can email some information. You always drop what you're doing and immediately email them what they want. This causes your partner some unhappiness (and rightly, some consternation!) when you two had been enjoying, say, a leisurely Sunday lunch. The reverse of this would be to ignore any incoming calls from work when you're supposedly off duty, and instead prioritising your relationship. But even better would be to tell your boss that you won't be available at the weekend unless it's been pre-arranged. That would help you to prioritise the important elements of your life, and keep all the balls flowing nicely. And in this example, this reverse response would undoubtedly increase your and your partner's levels of happiness.

Identify inflexible thinking: You can probably feel it coming on by now – that urge to reject anything other than what you normally expect. But even if you haven't been consciously aware of patterns of inflexible thinking, now's the time to start to identify them. This links in to what I've previously mentioned of that 'little devil on your shoulder' that chatters at you in a negative way. Does it also chatter at you about rejecting anything that might feel like it would create 'disequilibrium' for you? When actually it wouldn't necessarily be 'disequilibrium'? Learn to switch it off when it urges you to be inflexible. Instead switch on a confidence-boosting little angel that tells you that you can do something differently, that your priorities may need changing slightly or rejigging – and that you can address these and make sure your priorities stay balanced in a way that suits your changing life.

Your personality and having a healthy and happy realism

Another aspect of your personality that definitely can help you in balancing priorities and generally meeting challenges, as well as increasing happiness, is how realistic your outlook is to the world. How realistic you are in your approach to life is terribly important to your well-being. If you float about in some sort of fantasy world you'll almost always be disappointed. If you have completely unreal expectations about others and what they can or cannot do for you, or your work and what you can or cannot get out of it, or any other aspect of your life, again you'll be disappointed.

You might think, 'Hang on a minute, but what about all those creative day-dreamers who end up inventing something amazing or are very artistic, I bet they're not realists!' Creativity and inventiveness is not what I'm talking about here. Those are fantastic things and something *everyone* should make time for in their life. It shouldn't just be a painter or an inventor who gets to spend some of their time being incredibly creative and not worrying about the real world *as it is*. With the inventor, their thinking about how we can make the real world more exciting, fun or incredible is a good thing. And with the painter, thinking how they can make the real world perhaps a bit more beautiful is also a positive thing. What I'm talking about here, in your approach to the world being realistic, is about facing things head-on, blinkers off and eyes wide open. That means, say, if you really want to meet someone and settle down, and have just started dating someone new, you don't have over-the-top romantic fantasies that they'll sweep you off your feet, know what you're thinking, bring you fabulous gifts, and so on. That's just not realistic! That's a sugarcoated dream and a romantic fantasy.

Also having a healthy and happy realism doesn't mean the reverse, where you face life like Mr Burns in *The Simpsons*. You know the type of character – one who is extremely pessimistic and cynical, and always sees the worst. That is clearly 'doing down' what is usually the reality of someone's life.

Answer the following questions for a quick reality check

1. Do people accuse you of having your 'head in the clouds'?

      Yes   No

2. Has someone ever told you that you were 'avoiding the reality' of a situation?

      Yes   No

3. Do you find that you get lost in your daydreams?

      Yes   No

4. Has a partner ever told you that you've got unrealistic expectations for a relationship?

       Yes   No

5. Do you feel constantly let down by life despite the fact that your friends and family members lead fairly similar lives and don't seem to feel that way?

       Yes   No

6. Has anyone ever complained that 'nothing's ever good enough for you'?

       Yes   No

Your responses

Five or six 'Yes' answers

Lack of realistic outlook. Your answers suggest that you don't face the world with much realism. This can jeopardise your happiness in many ways, particularly because you'll usually be disappointed, whether you're expecting something profound to happen in your love life or something amazing to happen in your work life. Or any point in between where your expectations can be dashed. Yes, of course, wonderful things can happen from time to time, but such very high expectations aren't realised, across the board, much of the time. Try the suggestions below to enhance a more realistic outlook and increase your levels of happiness.

Three or four 'Yes' answers

Some lack of realistic outlook. Although some of the time you may have a realistic outlook on life and face things the way they are, you jeopardise your happiness because a good deal of the time you are unrealistic in your outlook. Do a 'reality check' and make sure you can tell the difference between realistic expectations and unrealistic ones when you're appraising a situation or person. Try the advice below.

Nought to two 'Yes' answers
A realistic outlook. Overall you have a realistic approach to life and that's extremely positive. Not only do you not over-egg the reality of a situation, but you're also unlikely to get lost in unrealistic expectations of more general things – the broader strands of life such as relationships. This has very positive implications for your happiness levels.

How to tackle unrealistic expectations

Run it past: If you're facing something that raises your expectations, consider running it past someone whose judgement you trust. So, for example, you've been single a while, you're going on a first date and you have incredibly high expectations for it. These expectations have led to lots of first-day nerves, self-doubts and less happiness about the impending date for that matter. This is the time to tell that person you trust what your expectations are and ask what they think about them. They may well talk you down from putting so much 'weight' onto one date. Hopefully you then go with a more relaxed attitude and actually enjoy yourself. Run any such situation, dilemma, doubts, and so on, past someone you think makes good decisions, who evaluates things well.

Ask for an explanation: If someone – friend, partner, colleague – challenges what your expectations are about something, use this as an opportunity to learn more about yourself and how you may be seeing things unrealistically. Ask them for an explanation *in detail* of what they mean. Why do they think your expectations are too high and unrealistic? Then consider the wisdom of their answer and see if it influences the way you feel and perhaps brings you back down to reality.

Real-life reality check: Think about a recent example where your expectations were not met. It can be a work or personal situation, but it should be one where you were absolutely aware that your expectations were not being fulfilled.

♦ On a piece of paper write down what your expectations were and how you were left feeling, for example, 'I expected my boss to give me much more praise for that piece of work than they did. That left me feeling disappointed and unhappy.'

♦ Next, write down what actually happened. What was said or done that didn't meet your expectations? In other words, the actual reality of the situation. In this example it might be, 'My boss made only a passing remark about a "good job".' Now you can examine the difference between what your expectations were and what actually happened. In this case you expected your boss to pause and make a specific comment about how great your work was.

♦ Next answer the question why you don't think your expectations 'happened'. Could your boss have been too busy to spend the time praising you? Could they have recently seen lots of good work of yours and already given you lots of praise? Could other colleagues have presented them with work of an even higher calibre and so yours didn't seem as good as you thought? Or maybe your boss just isn't very good at giving praise? Once you start doing a 'real life reality check' like this you can usually come up with about four or five reasons as to why your expectations weren't met. You still might think your expectations should have been met – but maybe not, and at least this can help you see the reality of many situations. And that many situations just aren't that straightforward.

24-hour pause: When you've started to anticipate something, or you've begun fantasising that some desire of yours is going to be met, or you can feel your expectations being raised, train yourself to sit on these feelings for 24 hours. Put them out of your head and relax about the situation. When you feel these thoughts beginning to emerge again, then force them to the back of your mind. Even imagine a little compartment in your mind specifically for high expectations. Visualise opening the door and waving these thoughts through to be contained and calmed in this compartment. Using this method can sometimes dampen down overly high expectations. You may find by the next day you've got things in perspective.

Five-second pause: It can become reflexive to express high – and potentially unrealistic – expectations, whether at work or with a partner, as soon as a 'trigger' subject comes up. By 'trigger' I mean anything that inspires a strong emotional response. When getting into that sort of territory during a conversation, be aware of this and give yourself a moment to pause and think before you speak. Obviously the saying 'think before you speak' became an old adage because its benefits are positive. And it's definitely true in these circumstances.

Your expectations for happiness and self-fulfilling prophecies

Our expectations have an enormous impact on what actually happens – and that includes what happens in terms of our happiness. This is important to consider because it can become a self-fulfilling prophecy when you expect certain things to happen. Your expectations influence everything you do. And this can become a positive cycle that increases your chance of having happiness, or a negative cycle that decreases your chance of happiness.

Let me give you a very clear-cut example. Let's say you wake up on the wrong side of bed because you've tossed and turned and start the day feeling exhausted. You immediately say to yourself, 'Uh oh, I can tell what kind of day this is going to be!' Your expectations are: this isn't going to be a good day and you're going to have a bad time of it. That expectation sets the tone for your whole day and it becomes a self-fulfilling prophecy.

You drag yourself into the shower, rush through breakfast and leave your home for work. Your train's late and you eventually slump into your chair as soon as you get to work. There you sit, thinking today is a miserable day because being late reconfirmed your original feelings from when you woke up. Later that morning a colleague thinks it would be nice to grab you for a coffee. They haven't seen you for a while and would love to catch up. As they enter your part of the building and begin to approach your desk they spot you slumped over papers and looking miserable. They have second thoughts, turn around and decide it's probably not a good time to approach you. Because your expectations get reflected in things like your facial expressions and body language, those around you can 'read' your negativity. Unless they have good reason to talk to you, they decide to avoid you. In this case, your day became bleaker – and lonely – because people gave you a wide berth. You go to bed that night and say to yourself, 'I'm so glad this day is over!'

What's the lesson from this? If you allow yourself to expect the worst, to expect unhappiness, and generally to be negative, then that will have profound implications for your BPH and cast a shadow over the important strands of your life. It will also have implications for your SPH as you'll fail to notice potential moments of happiness and joy in your day.

I've used a very simple example of how your expectations can colour all that you do. Believe me, they play themselves out even without you realising it. I'm sure you can think of a time where you decided not to approach someone because they looked annoyed or miserable. And expectations don't just cloud (or potentially improve things if they're positive) a situation you're in, your whole day, your relationship, your work, and so on. You can get entire 'group expectations' that can increase or decrease positive or negative feelings, attitudes and beliefs. This happens where a group of people, be they friends, family or colleagues, and so on, find their expectations feed off each other. What about a whole nation and its expectations? One American author claimed that the British weren't very happy as they looked at life as 'about *getting by* rather than being *about happiness*'.[11] Are your expectations of life that you're just going to get by? Or do you have higher expectations but still realistic ones?

I'm sure you can guess how important it is to balance 'one part expectations' with 'one part reality'! I've already made you aware of not having pie-in-the-sky, ridiculously high expectations. But equally now you can understand it's important to catch yourself when you're setting expectations too low, when, say, you've had something like a bad meeting or a bad date, or even something more profound that hijacks having positive expectations. Don't let these things cloud the rest of your day, your week or even your life. Remind yourself of the example above of the bad night's sleep and being late into work, and don't let such things set up expectations for the rest of your day that are gloomy. That's one surefire way of letting happiness slip through your fingertips.

Smaller Picture Happiness

We've considered some important things that impact on your happiness, such as aspects of your personality, flexible thinking, prioritising and finding balance, being aware of your expectations, and others, in terms of BPH. Now let's think about SPH in more detail.

Some people might think, 'What's the big deal?' about noticing the little things in our lives that make us laugh, make a moment joyful, or simply bring a smile to our face. I'll tell you what the big deal is, it's that much of life is difficult, there are all sorts of stresses and strains both big and small, there are challenges that test us, and others around us clamouring to get the things they want elbowing us out of the way no matter what the cost. To counter these things that test us, or can make us unhappy, are all those little things that often go unnoticed. And do you know why they go unnoticed? Because we can almost become unwittingly overwhelmed by the things that irritate, annoy, hurt and frustrate.

In speaking to countless people about their daily lives I regularly witness how those little 'negatives' of life chip away at our general well-being. So it's those little 'positives' that can redress this balance. Unfortunately we often fail to see them or allow them into our lives, when doing so would enhance our sense of well-being.

To bring this point home I think a study of lottery winners gives us an amazing example of the importance of SPH. This research found that what lottery winners enjoyed most was the freedom to *enjoy the things in life that are free.*[12] The winners highlighted things like a long soak in the bath, or a leisurely stroll in the park, as what they most enjoyed doing post-win. It wasn't staying in five-star luxury hotels or buying big cars that gave them the most happiness. Their money had freed them up so that they could now enjoy these simple pleasures without rushing. Despite having a good deal of money the winners still wanted to do the things that those without money wanted to do more of – but perhaps didn't have the time. Their lottery win had given them the luxury of having the time to do these things. Of course they were honest about how nice it was to have financial security, but interestingly, with that security seemed to come some wisdom. To paraphrase one lottery winner, 'You can have lots of money, but if you have no one to share it with it's simply numbers in the bank.'[13]

We don't really need lottery winners to teach us the lesson that material things and money aren't the route to happiness. Pick up any celebrity magazine – or even any newspaper for that matter –

and there have been endless stories over the years about the rich and famous who have ended up addicted to drugs, alcohol or sex, divorced, had affairs, and so on, and many other types of unhappy endings. You can have the biggest mansion in Beverly Hills but if you don't have important strands of BPH, like a good relationship and friends, plus a good measure of SPH and an awareness of the happy little things in your life, you could be utterly miserable.

Little creatures and large happiness

In fact a number of studies have shown how the simple pleasures of owning a pet can increase happiness. One such study found that merely walking your dog can cut your levels of stress and boost happiness.[14] For dog owners, getting out to walk their dogs gave them many simple pleasures, including being with their dog, of course; getting closer to nature; having some exercise; and the bonus of connecting with other dog walkers. Repeated studies have found that simple things like the act of petting your cat lead to an immediate sense of well-being. I know from my love of animals and having pets over the years just how true this is – my home is never without a couple of cats!

Some of your Small Picture Happiness directly links into the Bigger Picture Happiness of your life, as we shall see in Will's story.

Will's unhappy story

When you feel like you've 'lost it all', you'd think the little things would be the last thing on your mind. But let me use Will and his story to illustrate just that: how important the little things are to your happiness. This isn't a long story with lots of strategies to share with you that Will used to enhance his life, instead it simply illustrates this point perfectly.

Will, 31, had only been married to his wife Linda, 32, for three years when she had an affair. They'd had their daughter, now 3½ years old, in the first year of their marriage. They experienced the usual stresses and strains of a young couple with fledgling careers and a baby, but Will thought they were managing these well. He loved Linda deeply and was over the moon at becoming a father.

Linda, on the other hand, had issues in previous relationships over feeling bored and wanting 'more', and found these feelings developing in her marriage with Will. Instead of facing these feelings like a responsible and loving partner, Linda got involved with a married colleague. To cut a long story short, when Will discovered the affair he was devastated. Linda and her lover decided they were better suited to each other, and that they would throw away their marriages. She took the baby and set up home with this other man. Will was left with a broken heart and access rights of every other weekend plus Wednesday evenings.

Will's happy beginning

Once he got through the first couple of traumatic months, Will explained what continued to carry him through, as he rebuilt his life as a single father, with only part-time access. What got him through were the full access visits with his daughter *plus* the little moments he treasured between visits when he'd get to speak to her briefly on the phone each evening before bedtime. As he explained, he only had a couple of minutes because she was still such a young child, but to hear her laugh and her voice saying, 'Night

night, Daddy'. uplifted him and gave him more happiness
than he could imagine.

When you think about those moments Will shared with his
daughter, they were like extremely happy but tiny punctua-
tions between the bigger things they shared on access visits.
I think of them as like a little strand of fairy lights blinking
and brightening up his days. In fact Will said that one of the
biggest lessons he learned from his divorce was to treasure
the small moments. I think that's something we can all learn.

Little connections with loved ones

Research confirms the importance of little connections with loved
ones – like Will had with his daughter in their brief phone calls – in
your day-to-day happiness. Guess what one survey found out about
married women and what made them happiest? It found that they
valued a romantic dinner with their husbands over and above
anything else in giving them happiness.[15] I can completely understand that as I know how much I treasure a quiet dinner with my
husband (obviously not the one I divorced, but the lovely man I
married in 1995). And a little romance doesn't have to be about
going out to a 'romantic' restaurant – I say get out the candles and
put on some soft music when you're simply dining together at home.
You don't need an excuse for enhancing everyday connections to
loved ones with some simple details like candles and music.

There's a great big world out there
full of small pleasures

There's one thing I can guarantee you in a life where supposedly
there are no guarantees. And that's that you can *never* run out of
things that could potentially bring you SPH. It's not only, as we can
get from Will's story, that there are endless small moments of joy

and happiness to be found in your relationships, but also that there are endless possibilities out there in the big wide world.

Before we take a look at that, please make a note here of three examples of SPH from your immediate relationships:

1 ....

2 ....

3 ....

An important point was made in a report that simply having a new experience was claimed to stimulate happy feelings in people over and above material wealth.[16] Considering this report was made by a City analyst who specialises in the psychology and well-being of City workers, I think this is a pleasant surprise. You might expect that people working in finance would skew their happiness towards the accumulation of wealth! Just think about how people act when they've had a new experience – you hear exclamations of, 'Wow, I didn't know I'd enjoy that!' or, 'That was great!' and, 'I never knew *that* existed'. Whether 'that' was a newly discovered park, an old statue in a corner of a town square, an abseiling wall at the local gym, an exhibition at a local gallery – anything!

New experiences can cover a range of things from having taken your first-ever salsa dance class, to finding out you had an interest in wine tasting, to cooking a new recipe, to a first kiss with a new partner. They could include your first visit to an art gallery, the first time you smell a new scent, or meeting a new colleague. When you think about it that way, practically every day brings a new experience.

To keep your mind focused on this idea, write down your most recent new experience:

Don't get hung up with the big events

We're faced with vast numbers of options when it comes to the pursuit of new experiences and excitement. When you see advertised all around you amazing things, such as potentially taking holidays more suited to a James Bond film, or doing things like swimming with sharks, trekking the Inca Trail or visiting Cambodian jungles, then you can get wrapped up in the belief that the little things don't count. Those things certainly are marvellous adventures and I've walked the Inca Trail myself. However it's easy to feel hard done by if you don't have the resources for such things. We can get overtaken by a childlike response of, 'My best friend Jan trekked the Himalayas, so I want to!' That's a real happiness-killer.

It's easy to lose all proportion and forget what's on our doorsteps. So it's a good time to remember the simple pleasures that can be enjoyed. Keep in check your longings for the 'big event' when it comes to life experiences. Make a list of the little things you take for granted that might be on your doorstep, like a beautiful fountain in your local park, your local art gallery or a nearby beauty spot. Stroll past these little pleasures, sit and enjoy them. Even take your dog for a walk past them, seeing as you now know the health benefits of doing that.

The simplest of pleasures

Even doing the simplest things can sometimes bring pleasure and in turn increase happiness. This is why I don't want you to underestimate SPH. Because by developing your SPH, when you recognise and seize hold of moments of SPH every day it can become quite a powerful way to increase your levels of happiness. One study found that simply taking 10 minutes to meditate in a quiet room soothed people's minds and allowed them to absorb a certain calmness.[17] What could be simpler than that? A spin-off benefit of a simple 10-minute meditation is lower blood pressure. Yet we often don't even give ourselves 10 minutes to meditate quietly. I've already mentioned a number of visualisations to try in the last few chapters, and frequently I've said to just allow yourself a few moments to do so. Clearing your mind of stresses and strains, responsibilities and deadlines, and letting it refocus on visualising a pleasing scene can be calming as well as uplifting.

I may look daft but sometimes I just like to stop and stare at one of my cats stretching on our doorstep. Or perhaps it might look even stranger when I gaze at the sunset as I walk to the local shops. When was the last time you just stopped and stared for a moment at something with natural beauty like that?

List three simple pleasures you've enjoyed recently:

1 ....

2 ....

3 ....

Happiness Principle Four

Learn to embrace happiness on a smaller scale and it can increase happiness in the bigger picture.

It's often easier to start small – and think about increasing your Smaller Picture Happiness – than to worry about the big picture, as that can seem overwhelming at times. Taking little steps to enjoy unexpected moments of pleasure and joy can go a long way to improving all the strands of your life.

The power of humour to increase happiness

Nearly last, but certainly not least, when it comes to little mood-lifters and happiness boosters, psychologically about the best one is humour. There's been much research into humour and laughter and how it relates to happiness. One study found that simply watching an episode of a favourite sitcom like *Friends* made people happier almost instantly.[18] I've often recommended to people who are a bit down in the dumps to record some of their favourite sitcoms and enjoy a dose of laughter each evening. It really is the medicine that can cure a little slump in mood.

Generally speaking, humour and laughter serve a number of emotional and psychological functions. These include stress relief, because a good laugh actually helps to release endorphins – those feelgood brain chemicals. When these are released into your bloodstream they counteract feeling stressed. Humour and laughter are also a great form of social bonding. And if you've felt a bit distant from your partner or friends, then going out to see a comedy or watching one at home together can serve to reconnect you. Quite naturally, when you laugh together you stick together. Again this is something I recommend for couples who have been bickering and arguing – to actually laugh together over a comedy can help mend some ill feelings.

Enjoying an evening at a comedy club, or watching your favourite sitcom, or an old funny film on television, can also help deflect you temporarily from some of life's daily troubles. There's absolutely nothing wrong with taking time out from the things that worry you – in fact there's everything right about it.

Certainly one of the simplest ways to enjoy humour and a touch of happiness between you and a friend or partner is to email or text each other a joke. I have one friend who regularly sends me funny anecdotes, jokes and comedy clips by email and it always brings a smile to my face. That's certainly welcome in the middle of a busy day where it means I take a moment and have a little giggle. Also I know it means my friend has thought of me when she sends it and she knows that now I'll be thinking of her as I enjoy her email. That's got to be one of the easiest ways possible to keep connected and enjoy a happy moment.

Interaction of Bigger Picture Happiness and Smaller Picture Happiness

Throughout your life BPH and SPH can interact. Consider this example: let's say that during a particular phase of your life you had low levels of BPH because you'd lost your job and were experiencing all the uncertainty that situation brings with it. You moved from having a broad strand of good and high levels of BPH from your satisfying career, bolstered by a good relationship, to having a big part of that broad strand taken away. However let's say that you still maintained your relationship and tried not to let the upset over your career loss damage it. You also decided to make sure you embraced any small moments of happiness that came your way in terms of SPH. For example, you made a point of regularly grabbing a coffee with friends to stay connected to them between interviews for new jobs.

However if the loss of your job also impacted badly on your relationship, because for whatever reason you and your partner didn't handle the increased stress well, you may have found it hard to notice the small amounts of joy that arise in everyday life. You ignored that smiling child in the supermarket, or said 'No' to invitations to meet up with a friend to grab a coffee. In this case your SPH would be affected as badly as your BPH.

As I'm sure you can now guess, there are many, many potential ways your BPH and SPH can influence and affect each other. Increased awareness of this ongoing dynamic should help you maintain your levels of both. A great example of how this interacts in real life comes from a survey of young mothers.[19] Social isolation is a big problem for mothers of young children and in the first few years of their child's life they can be at their least happy. However it was found that the simplest things like turning off the TV, and getting out more and talking to others, were a big help in increasing their overall levels of happiness. So the broad theme of feeling isolated at home for a number of years – their BPH when their child is young – could be improved by SPH – getting out and enjoying small moments of happiness. Now I'd argue that most mothers of young children actually experience lots of moments of happiness with their children, but that these can sadly be overshadowed by the fatigue from sleepless nights and constantly being on the go with the demands of a baby or young child. This sense of being overwhelmed can be compounded by the lack of other adults to talk to over an entire day. Which is why this survey found that isolated mothers felt happier from the improved interaction with others – a simple solution.

I've now got you thinking about Bigger Picture and Smaller Picture Happiness. The Bigger Picture Happiness that forms the background on your canvas of life is crucial to your overall happiness. And those Smaller Picture Happiness brushstrokes that have the potential to lighten and brighten each day are also important.

I'd now like to talk about something crucial to your happiness – affecting the big picture and the smaller one – the emotional hole, or wound, that most humans carry within them and neglect to heal.

Build Your Happiness Habit

At the end of each day recall one happy moment from that day. Hold on to it briefly and enjoy reliving it.

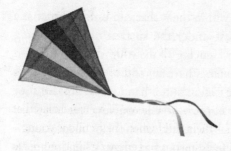

5

Happy Healing for the Walking Wounded

*It is only possible to live happily ever after on a
day to day basis.*

Margaret Bonnano

Have you ever had a sense of having some sort of emotional hole, right in the centre of your heart? Or maybe it's not in your heart so to speak, but you feel it right at the core of you, in the depths of your soul? And you might not feel it as a hole but you'd describe it as being more like a wound? Perhaps some sort of emotional scarring that fails to heal and underlies so much of what you do, what you feel, and generally how you experience your life.

You're definitely not alone. In fact I'd argue that every person has some sort of emotional hole or wound, even if for some it's only a small part of how they feel inside. It's still experienced as some sort of painful area within them that can bubble up at any time. For others it lies just under the surface of their waking experiences at all times, influencing all that they do.

But some would deny that they have any sort of emotional hole or wound. They'd dismiss the notion out of hand and claim that they feel whole and in one piece inside, thank you very much. I'd say they're in some sort of denial – whether conscious or unconscious – about how they really feel and what they've undoubtedly experienced. For those who deny that they've experienced these feelings, and still carry around some sort of emotional pain or scarring, end up actually harming their chances of healing their pain.

To be human is to have experienced hurt

I absolutely believe that everyone has been emotionally injured or wounded by something in their life. No human can escape emotional pain and the scarring that goes with it. You wouldn't be human if you hadn't been affected by some incident or general experience, even in your childhood. To be human is to be wounded in some way. And of course such emotional holes or wounds profoundly affect our happiness.

I say this based on the fact that in my life, both personal and professional, I have met all sorts of people from the cleaner to the captain of industry, from the shop assistant to the celebrity. When people open up in an honest way, every single one of them has experienced some sort of personal pain, trauma, upset, unhappy relationship or bad treatment by someone else. Many people manage fairly well, move on and hopefully heal in good measure, but still in their stories there's almost always an echo of the emotional pain that lurked within them.

This doesn't mean we're all terribly damaged and walk around enveloped in a heavy cloud of emotional pain. We aren't all weeping behind closed curtains or unable to get out of bed to face the reality of our lives. Yes, there are those who are so severely traumatised or damaged that they do spend much of their time in extreme emotional pain and are unable to get up and face the day. But for many of us, we continue to heal, get by, or at least appear to those around us to manage our pain.

Sometimes that great big emotional hole is so painful that a person gets to a point of feeling numbed by it. Or they simply feel 'empty', as if they've been drained by the experience of having carried emotional pain around. It's been a burden or weight that they've carried for far too long. They also know that they're drained of all the wonderful, nurturing emotions that they'd love to be filled up with, like love, care and respect. Whether it's numbness or an empty hole they experience, it's still there, reminding them of enduring unhappiness.

Before we go any further I want to make the point now that I'm hitting on some terribly important and really quite vast areas that influence human pain, and the choices we make in response to pain. As *Happy Human* is about the 10 Happiness Principles it means that, as I pointed out previously, I can only hope to touch upon and explore the issues most relevant to each Principle. At the very least I hope this stimulates self-examination, and a decision to change anything you feel should change in the light of each Principle as it applies to your life. And finally I'll offer some relevant, do-able advice that will help you on your way.

What is the source of our emotional pain?

There are so many potential sources of emotional pain. The main culprits that truly wound people are unhappy childhood experiences. Such experiences range from the extreme, to the not so extreme that can still have lasting effects. On the extreme side, people may have been caused enormous unhappiness when their parents didn't, couldn't, or wouldn't love and nurture them. In less extreme cases they've experienced difficult circumstances like the divorce of their parents, fragile economic circumstances, parents who had problems with alcohol or drugs, or simply parents who *un*intentionally didn't 'parent well'.

Or the reason behind their pain may have nothing to do with their family life and comes from a different source, like experiencing a trauma, or having unhappy, perhaps abusive relationships. They may have failed at a job at a critical time of their emotional development, which leaves them with a legacy of unhappiness. They might even have been hurt by a so-called friend who turned out to offer only a toxic, destructive friendship. The source of unhappiness can come in many shapes and forms, and I've heard stories from people who were surprised by the experiences, incidents, and even the people that have crossed their paths and for one reason or another ended up causing them unhappiness. As you can see, and I'm sure from your own experience you know this, people can be let down and hurt in any number of ways.

Why don't we heal more easily?

We as humans have a terrific capacity for coping with difficult and changing conditions, and the challenges and hurdles of life. However there are some things that hurt us in such a way, or at a particular time in our lives when we might be more vulnerable, that we find harder to heal. We move on from the situation, lick our wounds and hope for the best. Or maybe even stay put, as is the case where people get stuck in abusive relationships. But very often the source of pain sits under the surface and isn't healed properly and fully.

We might push it to one side, with that human optimism, and cross our fingers that all will be well. If life was simple, then time with its healing powers would probably be enough to sort us out and see us through. However, life is complicated and we inevitably find we're confronted with another difficult situation, another hurtful episode in a relationship, or anything else that bruises us a bit more or maybe even batters us emotionally. That next negative experience lays down another level of pain, on top of the original hurts and past pains that haven't fully healed. You can understand how these things start to mount up and old wounds get ripped open again, scars that are starting to form get broken, and this cycle continues.

Your emotional resilience

You might well think that in between the hurts, the rifts and challenges of life there are also the good things that happen to us – and so ask why they don't hasten our healing, speeding up the whole process so that we're complete again? It's down to your basic emotional resilience and how this ebbs and flows and has peaks and troughs over the years. Your emotional resilience is an overall sense of how good you feel about yourself generally, how you tend to cope with things, and your general levels of happiness compared to unhappiness.

Let me explain this by giving you a simple analogy: think of your emotional resilience like a bank balance. Your balance can be a healthy one, at a high level, that pushes it into the black. Or it can be an unhealthy one, at a lower level, that pushes it into the red. Just as your bank balance varies when it comes to your money – it has its ups and downs throughout your life – so too does your balance of emotional resilience.

Why do I feel more emotional pain than others?

It's a trap we fall into when we compare ourselves to those we know and we decide that we have more pain – and with it more unhappiness – than others. You can never really know how someone else truly feels inside. The colleague that you judge to be happier than you may be better at covering up any hurt or pain that they harbour. Or they might genuinely be happier, or are going through a happier phase in their life. It's the same with a friend or family member, and even a partner – people aren't always completely honest about their state of mind or level of well-being.

The point is, there's *no point* in comparing yourself and your levels of emotional resilience and happiness to what you think others are experiencing. Ask yourself what you can gain from that? If you judge them to be happier than you are, will that lead to envy on your part? Or will you feel good for them? Does that make any difference to your happiness? Not one jot! But unfortunately you might let it – if you feel envy, and you allow that envy to cut you up inside.

What if you judge them to be less happy than you? Again, does that really impact on your well-being and sense of emotional resilience? Hopefully you wouldn't gloat inside about them going through an unhappy phase. But I know human behaviour and I know that many people *would do so*. Again, you need to explore where such feelings like gloating about someone else's unhappiness come from and how they might actually damage you.

Making Unhelpful Comparisons

Make a note here of the last time you found yourself judging someone else's levels of unhappiness in comparison to your own. What was the situation?

✎ ....

In your heart of hearts, how did that really make you feel? Guilty about gloating? Pleased that you felt you were better off? Did you feel concern for their situation? Or did you envy their happiness?

✎ ....

If you did feel in any way 'good' about someone else being unhappier than you, I hope you'll consider this: feeling good about someone else's unhappiness, a person that presumably you know and like, will *never* lead to real happiness within you. Because what this implies is that there's something inside you that's eating away at your well-being, leaving you wanting to see others suffer in some way. As I said, it's quite human and normal to have these feelings, but that doesn't mean they are healthy feelings to have – they can damage your happiness. And definitely I've found that in those who are happier, such feelings are only fleeting and very rare.

It's important to your well-being and happiness to be aware of when you feel good that someone else feels bad. Awareness of such impulses and feelings can help you respond in a way that ensures you can feel good about your own situation without feeling good that someone else is in a difficult situation. Don't forget that such feelings should flag up to you that there must be something negative underlying them. That in actual fact you're not all that happy – and better off than they are – if you feel good about their difficult situation.

Where does such emotional pain lead us?

Thinking of the pain and hurt that we carry within us, to one extent or another, leads me to the critical point of this chapter. Where does this pain lead us? What do we end up doing and how do we end up acting because of it? We often end up behaving and acting in a number of destructive ways to combat emotional pain. At first this sounds contradictory. You'd imagine people would try to do good things and behave in positive ways to try and heal their pain. Very often that's absolutely not the case! In fact, for many people, the path they choose to take when in pain is the one that brings them *even more pain*. And this leads to increasing levels of unhappiness. This is due to many things including :

♦ **denial** – because they hide their pain from others.
♦ **powerlessness** – because they feel they don't have the power to do something to change it.
♦ **guilt and shame** – because they are ashamed and/or feel guilty about their situation.
♦ **isolation** – because they feel isolated and believe there's no one to turn to.
♦ **lack of knowledge** – because they actually don't know what to do, or what to try, to heal themselves.
♦ **escapism** – because they think they can 'escape' from their pain in many different ways. All of the above can lead to escapism.

Let me touch on these briefly in turn. A number of healing strategies will come later in this chapter.

Denial

At the beginning of the chapter I mentioned denial and how some people choose to shove their emotional pain so far into the depths of their psyche that they can ignore it. Or at least they think they can. Emotional pain and hurt have a way of resurfacing when least expected, particularly when you've been trying to deny them.

Alexandra's experience

Alexandra, 29, had been in an abusive relationship in her late teens and early 20s. Emotional abuse finally gave way to physical abuse. Eventually Alexandra, with the encouragement of family, left her boyfriend and moved on. She dated casually but never got involved with anyone until her late 20s when she met Philip. As they grew closer and started sleeping together Alexandra started to get strange feelings that made her feel 'weird'. She'd get a funny feeling in her stomach that made her feel a bit sick. They continued to grow closer – and these feelings became more frequent, until one day Alexandra broke up with Philip, leaving him absolutely stunned.

Until Alexandra started to truthfully explore what had happened, she denied that this was in any way related to her unhappy, abusive relationship in her early 20s. However, when she felt emotionally strong enough to be honest about her deepest feelings, Alexandra revealed that she harboured a painful sense of not being 'good enough' to receive real and genuine love. She'd been in denial about the emotional wound that had been left festering since that abusive relationship.

Maybe Alexandra's experience rings some sort of bell with you. Maybe almost inexplicably at some point your happiness was jeopardised by emotional pain you had previously denied and ignored. I have great news for you – it's never too late to start healing.

Powerlessness

I listed other important reasons why people don't try to heal themselves and instead often choose the route that turns out to be more damaging. These include a sense of powerlessness – where something has left you hurting, and feeling you don't have the power to overcome that hurt. Many people have described to me a sense that all their emotional energy has been sapped by, say, a destructive relationship or a traumatic event, and they end up feeling powerless to heal. This can be daunting to overcome. I see it as a 'trick of the mind' to feel that you don't have the power to make the situation better. *We humans have so much emotional power!* And I know of so many cases where someone has felt this way, only to discover that in actual fact they do have the power to overcome the pain they feel.

Guilt and shame

These are powerful emotions that can cause you terrible anxiety if left festering. They relate to your sense that somehow you're a damaged or tarnished person, perhaps because of escapist behaviours of your own – like having repeated, inappropriate sexual encounters. Or they relate to how someone has made you feel, as in Cathy's experience.

Cathy's experience

Cathy, 32, was sexually assaulted at a party. The fact that it happened to be by someone she knew slightly made her feel dreadful. She blamed herself and felt that she must have led him on in some way. Cathy feared telling anybody because she felt so ashamed, and also she worried that maybe she wouldn't be believed. This experience haunted her and she showed symptoms of PTSD – Post-Traumatic Stress Disorder. Cathy would get flashbacks and panic attacks when finding herself alone at social gatherings. She experienced sleeplessness and lots of anxiety. Despite all these symptoms the shame kept her from seeking help for two years.

Cathy finally confided in a friend what had happened, because her friend had been asking her why she was having panic attacks. Thankfully her friend encouraged her to go for counselling. Eventually Cathy let go of the shame she had felt, grew in confidence, and stopped having PTSD-type symptoms.

Unfortunately, many people let shame – of all types of hurts, wounds and pain – keep them from healing, and instead they are held like a prisoner in a dark and shadowy emotional corner.

Isolation

For other people it's a sense of feeling isolated from others, whose support they'd like or wish they had, that leaves them believing they can't face their emotional pain on their own. Sometimes people in this situation are genuinely isolated from others and feel very alone. Other times they perceive themselves as being isolated and think that people that, say, they work with or even have as friends, aren't close enough to want to help them. Or they wouldn't be interested in supporting them. They might well be wrong with these perceptions. And this means they isolate themselves further from people who'd actually happily lend an ear to their story or a shoulder to cry on.

Lack of knowledge

Sometimes with the best will in the world people who want to close old wounds or heal emotional pain simply don't know where to start. They've never picked up a self-help book that might have given them strategies to try, as this one does. They don't know who to ask about counselling or where they should begin.

Escapism

Now we come to the fascinating – and potentially huge – area of escapism. So many paths from unhappiness lead to escapism. And escapism can take many different forms, but here are some classic ones:

- alcohol and/or drug abuse (illegal and prescription drugs)
- risk-taking and inappropriate sexual behaviour
- comfort and/or binge eating, or withholding food from yourself, or purging and vomiting
- reckless and destructive behaviour in relationships – both personal and professional

◆ binge spending, problems handling money, and/or with gambling

Escapist behaviours have three main things in common:

1. All of these behaviours, at the outset, make a person feel 'better'. They feel better because for at least a time they can forget about their emotional pain. A few too many drinks blot out heartache. A binge on junk food eases emotional hurt. Reckless behaviour feels exciting – the antithesis of painful feelings.

2. These behaviours always eventually make matters worse! You might be able to get away with some excessive drinking, a few inappropriate sexual flings, or a handful of episodes of destructive behaviour in a relationship, but the escapism doesn't last. Ultimately things become more complicated, more painful, and harder to solve.

3. Finally, all escapist behaviours change the way you feel. They alter your brain chemistry, giving you sensations that you find irresistible and/or compelling. These sensations can become addictive. However, *Happy Human* isn't a book about addiction, so I'm not going into this important subject in more detail. I urge you to seek proper help if any of your escapist behaviours have tipped over into an addiction or are heading that way.

Negative, escapist behaviours also absorb any positive energy within you that could lead towards a happier life. What's important is to open your eyes to how any escapist behaviour you may use only temporarily masks your emotional pain and only camouflages your emotional hole. It will still be there, growing larger and requiring more feeding with even greater escapist behaviours.

Then your anger creeps in

Another offshoot of emotional pain, particularly when someone has been using escapist behaviour to avoid it, is unresolved anger. Harbouring anger and rage can be highly damaging.[20] One study that looked at anger and rage generally, rather than in terms of how it relates to escapist behaviour, found that these seem to feature more and more in our society, with one in three people stating it's a chronic problem either for them or for someone close to them. That's a whole lot of anger!

Of course that anger can be directed at those around you – or at yourself. When it's directed at yourself, and combined with escapist behaviour, it becomes a very nasty cycle. You might ask why people start getting angry with themselves when they're using escapism – often it's because they quickly realise what they're doing is damaging, destructive and even dangerous. They know they shouldn't be doing it and so they become very angry with themselves.

As with other powerful emotions, anger can be a vital and important feeling. But there's only a positive outcome when people act on it by trying to solve the issues at the root of the anger. At the root lies much emotional pain that having an angry outburst isn't going to solve. Instead that anger needs to be directed in a controlled and monitored way.

 What's your escapism of choice?

Whether it's drugs, alcohol, food, inappropriate sexual behaviour and so on, you need to face up to any escapist behaviour. Answer these key questions to determine if you use escapist behaviour/s.

1. Do you go out expressly to 'get drunk', 'get high', and so on?

     Yes   No

2. Have you regretted any sexual contact that you've had?

  Yes   No

3. Have you behaved in a destructive manner in any of your relationships?

  Yes   No

4. Do you keep secret certain behaviours around food, alcohol, drugs, and so on?

  Yes   No

5. Do you find the only way to get peace of mind is to do something (like get drunk) to make you forget your troubles?

  Yes   No

Your responses

Answering 'Yes' to *any* of these questions suggests that you indulge in escapist behaviours. Also, if none of these questions apply specifically to your behaviour, but you do worry about such behaviour, this should cause you some concern. Here are some solutions.

Let's begin the happy healing

Embrace Your Unhappiness: As I said in the introduction to *Happy Human*, unhappiness is terribly important. It's important to help us understand our immediate world and what's important in that world, and what potentially causes us pain. Unhappiness helps us monitor the ups and downs of our lives, because through the flow of unhappy moments and times, happy moments and times, and all points in between, it gives us a message. It's also important because it helps us appreciate happiness even more when it comes our way. And we learn from it the strategies and solutions that put it right, and we can use these in future. It shouldn't be ignored, run from or denied. Instead I urge you to embrace your unhappiness. Literally wrap your arms around it and *feel it*. Know it and understand it and then you can act to improve it. It's far better to claim it and roll with it, than to do things like using escapist behaviours to try and avoid it. Sweep it under the carpet and it lurks there. Stare it straight in the eye and you can solve or heal it.

When was the last time you felt unhappy?

✎ ....

What did you do about it? (even if your answer is 'I did nothing')

✎ ....

If you did do something, was that to confront what was making you unhappy, or run from it with escapist behaviour?

✎ ....

Don't deny 'me': One method I've found that helps people heal their pain is to give it a 'shape' or to label it – even name it. That way it becomes more real and less likely that you'll deny it. Imagine giving shape to it, like a big dark cloud. Or name it the way Winston Churchill named his depression the 'black dog'. When you give it a shape, or name it, then it becomes something you have to do deal with. It literally says to you 'don't deny me'. Recent research now suggests that even when it comes to something as profoundly unhappy as experiencing a real depression or depressive episode, it's better to face it, and if possible to embrace it and work with it, without medication where appropriate, and you can come out the other side feeling emotionally stronger.[21, 22]

Transformative power of talking: Don't isolate yourself when you're unhappy and/or know that emotional pain haunts you.

Talking can transform the way you feel. Reach out to those you care for, and/or who care for you, and let them know you're going through a rough patch. Or be honest and tell them if you've decided to work to heal a long-existing emotional hole. Usually shame or fear of rejection is what stops someone from letting on that they're feeling unhappy. And, yes, sometimes when we ask for help we face rejection for whatever reason. The person we ask may simply not feel able to help us. If for any reason someone does reject you in this context, that will feel tough. But in the long run you'll know that they weren't really a friend or someone you could rely on.

If you feel isolated from others, for whatever reason, then explore whether your place of work offers a confidential counselling service, or if your GP practice has a practice counsellor. If they don't, they'll be able to refer you to someone. It's important, when you recognise emotional pain, that if it's a challenge greater than something you can rise to, you don't feel unable to seek professional help. *To ask for help is a sign of strength, not weakness.*

When it's right to bottle it up

Having just told you to use the transformative power of talking about your troubles, that's not always the best choice. I'm going to extrapolate from some research showing that in times of drama or trauma those who maintain a traditional stiff upper lip seem to be less affected by the trauma than those people who get more emotional.[23] This certainly gives food for thought. And in my experience sometimes those who heal their emotional pain don't allow themselves to crumble in the face of every hurdle. By willing themselves to find more strength in facing fresh struggles, they gain the confidence to continue healing old hurts.

Identify your emotions

Get into the habit of identifying your emotions. I've already mentioned earlier how important it is to know what you're feeling. You'd be surprised how many people are 'cut off' from their emotions. Unfortunately when you cut yourself off from your emotions it usually goes hand-in-hand with denial and escapist behaviours.

Make it a point to regularly – ideally on a daily basis – stop when you feel any emotion (whether positive or negative) and say to yourself, 'I feel angry, frustrated, bored, happy, anxious, flirtatious', and so on.

Note here one emotion you felt today:

✎ ....

Identify your emotional triggers

I've previously mentioned how certain triggers will set off particular responses. This is particularly true with the powerful emotions that go hand in hand with emotional hurt and pain. One of the key things you can do to ensure you embrace and challenge your emotional pain is to identify what sets off these feelings. Because it's once these feelings have been ignited – whether daily or only occasionally – that they have the power to send you running for alcohol, drugs, food, sex, and so on.

Think about the last time you tried to 'feed' your emotional hole with escapist or damaging behaviours. What were you thinking or feeling as you took that extra drink, binged on junk food, or searched the internet for a sexual fling? Make a note here:

✎ ....

What alternative behaviours could you have tried? For instance, ringing a friend for comfort, facing the person that upset you head on, and so on:

 ....

Remember there are always alternatives that you can try. You have the power to heal your emotional pain without self-destructive behaviours and in doing so you increase your levels of happiness.

A day at a time

You might recall when I discussed *not* viewing life as a rehearsal in Chapter Three. This theme is particularly important when healing emotional pain. It's no good living each day as if the unhappy things that have gone before will happen again today. When you do that you set up the expectation that you'll never escape your unhappiness. It's also no good living each day fearing what's going to happen tomorrow – or at any other point in the future. Yes, we must plan for our future, but that's very different to living in fear of it. Overall the best way to move forward with emotional pain is to conduct our lives on a day-to-day basis in a way that doesn't jeopardise our future.

This means you must stop yourself worrying that just because you were unhappy yesterday, and the day before that, you're necessarily going to be unhappy today and tomorrow. You need to seize hold of such thinking and say to yourself, 'I'm only focusing on today!' You can also vow, 'Today I'll do what I can to heal myself and make this the best possible day that I can experience!'

Happiness Principle Five

It's important to accept that you are only human, and to be human is to experience emotional pain. Learn to recognise any pain that exists within you and don't run from it.

You can slowly heal any emotional hole inside of you. Don't fool yourself that you're abnormal or different from others because of your pain. You are not different and you are not alone.

The key myths that lock us into our pain

There are many myths that hold us back from healing. Learn to recognise if you're buying into any of the following key myths. They only feed into any emotional pain you have and lead you down the path of unhappiness. Here are some classic ones:

I don't feel 'good enough' compared to others. Why wouldn't you feel as good as another person? What makes another person so good, amazing, admirable, better than you, and so on, in your mind? What in your heart makes you compare yourself unfavourably, not feeling 'good enough'? Don't judge yourself more harshly than you'd judge others. If you do, it's one sign of existing pain.

Other people seem to be happier than I am. Trust me, those 'others' who supposedly feel so much happier than you do probably don't feel any better than you. As I've already pointed out, it's no good to compare yourself in this way to others anyway. Rather than compare yourself, heal yourself.

I feel a fraud and a fake. It might make you feel uncomfortable, unpleasant or even downright bad to pretend to others that everything's OK in your world. Feeling that you're being a fraud is very demoralising. I can assure you that everyone who's walked this world has at sometime – if not regularly – put on a front of happiness and contentment so that others don't know how they're really feeling. This is absolutely human! It only becomes dysfunctional when you put on a fake front for those who should care about you. When you can't be genuine and truthful with them, then you need to question why you pretend one thing to them when you're feeling another.

Other people aren't lonely the way I am. Don't believe for a minute that, if you're lonely, others don't share that unpleasant emotional state with you. Recent figures suggest that there are more people living on their own than ever before and this is going to increase.[24] Yes, of course, many people who live on their own are perfectly happy and content, and lead fulfilling lives where they're connected to other people. Many, though, don't feel connected to others and living on their own compounds their sense of isolation and loneliness.

 HAPPY FACT: *A study in America found that those earning over $10 million were only slightly happier than those earning the national average.*

Continuing the happy healing

Here are some other strategies to try:

You always have a choice: No matter how you feel, and what type of escapist behaviours you might be doing, you always have a choice to do things differently, to live life in another way. Think about your choices in relation to your emotional pain. Let's say that you've been putting on a front to your loved ones, drinking too much, and lying about how you are to those who ask. Look at how many alternative choices you have to behave in a different way. You can be more open and honest with your loved ones. You can refrain from drinking or only drink limited amounts. You can let your guard drop a little bit at a time. You'll also have choices, though, about how to heal yourself. You might decide you'd like to try counselling. Or you might decide you simply need to put into practice living by the 10 Happiness Principles. You might decide that there's someone in your life who causes you too much pain and you need to re-evaluate that relationship ('your relationships and happiness' is coming in the next chapter). And perhaps you need to relate with them in a different way, set boundaries between you, and not absorb their negativity. Or it might be that you decide to change paths with your studies or career.

The wastage of worry: I would like you to name me one time when worrying about something helped you to solve it. I'm sure you can't actually name a time when fretting and worrying was actually a positive choice. Instead when you're experiencing pain, or harbouring an old wound, worrying about the circumstances around it takes away from your potentially *healing* energy. I've already asked you in previous chapters to switch off the negative little devil that might sit on your shoulder – the one that chatters at you in a negative, destructive way. This applies to worrying thoughts too. You have the power to challenge them and change them. Do this by reminding yourself of a recent time when you spent precious time worrying. Talk yourself through what this *didn't* do for the situation. Switch your worrying thoughts off and instead think about possible solutions and soothing thoughts that it'll be OK.

Positive reflections: Looking at your reflection in a mirror can be difficult when you've experienced unhappiness or are harbouring an emotional hole. This is because you often feel like a fraud, as I've mentioned, and don't want to look yourself in the eye. From my experience, when you feel like that, you'll look at your reflection with a critical eye. You don't really see a likeable person in the reflection. When that happens you know you need to start developing an appreciation for that person – you – reflected in the mirror. Look at yourself and 'calm' any negative feelings or thoughts you have about yourself. Try to find one good thing to say about yourself – perhaps that your face looks kind or that your eyes sparkle. Each day, as you go through your morning and evening routines, and have to look at your reflection in the mirror, remind yourself of this.

Your emotional inventory: Why not do an inventory of your emotional responses as you would do an inventory at your place of work? Doing an emotional inventory can be extremely constructive and help clarify how much of the time your emotional pain influences you and how much of the time it doesn't. Keep a notepad or dicta-phone by your side and when you get emotional about something – whatever it is – make a note. Do this for a minimum of two days, but preferably for a week. At the end of the time, count up the number of times you have experienced each major emotion – from feeling loving, happy, excited, and so on, to the difficult emotions like anger, jealousy, shame, bitterness and envy. What is the balance between the positive/happy emotions and your negative/unhappy emotions? Let this serve as a guide to how urgent it is that you look at any emotional hole honestly in order to start healing.

Secrets make you sicker: Many years ago I coined the phrase 'secrets make you sicker' because of the vast numbers of people I spoke to who became increasingly unhappy the longer they held secrets from loved ones, and/or the more secrets they had. By secrets I mean the things you do that are potentially self-destructive and damaging as well as the things you think and feel that are painful. In some ways this links into what I've said about denial and in other ways it links into my thoughts on being a fraud. Partly you keep emotional and behavioural secrets because you deny that they're really so important that you need to share them. And partly you keep them because you're ashamed of them. It's time to start sharing your secrets so they no longer feel like frightening, dark things in your private 'cupboard' of emotions. It's often easier to start telling a loved one about something you're secretive about in the present. For instance, you could disclose that you know you're drinking too much right now. It's then easier to work backwards and share secrets from your past that have been eating away at you. Learning to live more honestly with those you trust, love and share time with is very healing.

Find the optimist in you: It's a fact that optimists live longer than pessimists.[25] It's also true that if you can see the brighter side of things you tend to be happier. Of course it's your prerogative to think you'll never heal from any emotional pain you have. Or you can tell yourself, 'Yes, I'm going to be optimistic about today and my future.' We're back to 'choice' again – and the choice is yours to become a cup-half-full person as opposed to a cup-half-empty one.

Create your own comfort zone

Many people end up in escapist and harmful behaviour like bingeing on comfort food, excessive drinking, or inappropriate sex, to fill that emotional black hole inside them. Instead, why not create a comfort zone around you that cushions and cocoons you against the challenges of life. Here's how to create your own comfort zone:

Your imaginary cocoon: Visualise your comfort zone being like a cocoon that wraps around you and protects you. In this cocoon you feel safe, you experience self-love, self-respect, and you know you'll look at all your choices from the place of security. You have the power to construct a safe cocoon around you that optimises your potential to be happy and understand unhappiness.

Your environment: Making your environment hospitable and cosy strengthens your comfort zone. If things are chaotic you'll feel stressed and look to escapist behaviours to soothe your frazzled nerves. Tidy things up and streamline one room at a time. Then use some calming colours in key places, like where you sit and eat. Warm earth tones, pale pinks and yellows, but not over-bright yellows, are good for mood. Even if you can't stretch to redecorating, buy some throws or accent cushions in these colours – or those you find soothing.

Soothing sounds and scents: Every aspect of your environment is part of your comfort zone. Music has a powerful effect and can help conjure up happier emotions. Keep to hand a favourite CD or iPod full of good tunes to balance your mood. Use lavender or ylang ylang essential oils and/or candles to give off a calming fragrance.

Self-care: Within your comfort zone you'll make the right choices when it comes to eating healthy food, getting as much rest as you need, and doing things like drinking only in moderation. Self-care is something you should practise every day of your life.

Your comfort zone goes where you go

You need to carry your comfort zone – or your cocoon – with you wherever you go. Imagine it being wrapped around you, giving you security and comfort in any situation.

Having created your comfort zone it's important to maintain and nurture it. Let it be your safety net that stops you from using escapist behaviours or denying emotional pain.

I hope you have an understanding of how all of us – to one extent or another – have an emotional hole or painful emotional wound within us. I hope you'll start to heal yours. That's far better than falsely 'feeding it' with destructive things or ignoring it.

Don't forget:

♦ Identify your emotional pain.
♦ Explore where it comes from.
♦ Embrace it and claim it as yours – don't run from it.
♦ Then you can begin to heal.

It's now time to look at your relationships and the happiness and/or unhappiness they have the potential to bring you.

Build Your Happiness Habit

Nothing in life is set in stone, including your emotional unhappiness. So each day chip away at emotional pain, by doing things that heal you.

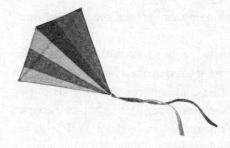

6

How to have Happy and Healthy Relationships

Those who bring sunshine into the lives of
others cannot keep it from themselves.

James M. Barrie

We can't help but be touched by other people, and it's our relationships with others that often hold the key to our most basic levels of happiness or unhappiness. As the saying goes, no man or woman is an island, and no one could claim that others don't influence how they feel across every level and on a day-to-day basis. Our relationships affect us in practically every possible way: not only in our basic levels of happiness, but also in how we view ourselves, our self-esteem and belief, and how we want to spend our precious time – whether with a particular person or not. Others profoundly affect our feelings in areas like rejection or acceptance, sense of belonging, of betrayal even, our sense of security, and so on.

In many ways we've touched on our relationships already. For instance, in Chapter One we looked at the Happiness Principle involving our parents – and a couple of main effects of that relationship on our happiness *even as adults*. In Chapter Three we looked at the Happiness Principle of how to claim our lives as our own, including not letting others run our lives. Now I'm going to present a number of themes that are important across your relationships – whether personal or professional. I'll also look at key elements specific to particular types of relationships – romantic, friendship, family, and work.

One study of happiness threw up some interesting conclusions about how crucial our relationships are to happiness.[26] Researchers found a few key things:

♦ Those people we'd consider to have the top careers and to be high achievers had moderate levels of happiness.
♦ They were more likely to earn more, and achieve more highly, than those who related themselves as very happy. So you might be happy working hard, but even happier when you find a balance between work and relationships.
♦ Those who rated themselves as *completely satisfied* tended to have more friends and stable relationships. Again, the happiest are those who put relationships over and above things like high achievement.

The results of this and other such research don't surprise me in the slightest. Your relationships are critical to your well-being and happiness. Ask yourself, when was the last time you were unhappy? and it probably has something to do with another person.

I'd like to introduce some major themes influencing your relationships and how happy they are – or aren't.

The 'script' you live and relate by

The theme of 'scripts' will arise in a few contexts. The main script of your life can be thought of as the role you play in relating to others. This is usually an unconscious role you're not necessarily aware of that plays itself out in your relationships. Your script emerges within your family life as a child, where you begin to fulfil certain expectations. Let's say you're the first child and so your parents invest many of their dreams in you. Your mother dreams you'll become a doctor. Your father dreams you'll become prime minister. Perhaps you're the baby of your family, and when speaking about you to one of your siblings, your parents refer to you as 'your little sister', or 'your little brother', and you have all those expectations that go with being the 'little one' or the 'baby' of the family. Another script found in most families is the 'scapegoat' – the naughty one – and anything you do will be seen as a result of your naughtiness.

We carry these scripts with us throughout our life and they affect all of our relationships in one way or another. We continue to play out our role and can be drawn to people who allow us to play this role, and be, for example, the baby, or the naughty one, or the successful one, and so on, in that relationship. However, playing out our scripts can squash our spirit, causing much unhappiness because these roles were *given to us* and aren't necessarily representative of us. They don't fulfil our capabilities and they keep us in a scripted straitjacket.

Does this ring any bells with you? Can you identify the family script that plays itself out in your life now? What would you identify as your role within your family, for instance, the naughty one, the clever one, the performer/clown, and so on?

 ....

Self-fulfilling prophecy

I've already written of the power of your will and how what you think about yourself is likely to come true. It affects what you do. In fact, when we have a repetitive thought, like 'I'm not good at relationships', that easily becomes a self-fulfilling prophecy. Self-fulfilling prophecies play into our scripts and they have a major impact on the way we relate to others. They can spring from our experiences, and often our negative self-fulfilling prophecies arise from a crisis. For instance, we can hold onto something that someone says and it will influence our future relationships. Sometimes – usually at a particular juncture in our lives like during a crisis, or when we feel vulnerable, or when we're looking to someone else for guidance – we're told something about ourselves (or we even tell ourselves something) that sticks with us.

Let's take an example where you always choose dominant partners and you play a submissive part in your relationships. Maybe your family script dictated that you were submissive, the one that always did as you were told. Your dominant partner tends to shout things like 'You're useless, not much good'. That can stick with you at a conscious level where you repeat this message to yourself, or it filters down into your unconscious mind. Even there it haunts you and can drive you towards fulfilling this message.

Always be on guard that you don't live out any negative self-fulfilling prophecies, and that what you've thought about yourself – or been told by another – isn't allowed to become a self-fulfilling prophecy in all of your relationships. Because if you allow the false sense of you being 'useless and not much good' to go through into one relationship after another, then you're likely to behave in ways that take your power away – and fulfil this prophecy.

What's your 'fallback position'?

The notion of self-fulfilling prophecies ties in with what I called your 'fallback/default position' when I discussed the blame game in Chapter One. It also links in with my thoughts on emotional, habitual behaviours. Your default position develops when at some point in the past it worked for you. So let's say you had a rather bullying partner or boss, and you found that if you withdrew emotionally, went quiet, and didn't argue your case, then it all went away and they were happy. Then that withdrawal behaviour becomes your fallback position in future when you're under pressure in a relationship. You felt that it worked for you in the past and so it feels quite natural to do it again in future. But what I'd like you to consider is that it *didn't* actually work for you. Instead it meant that you're easily bullied into what another person wants to do.

Have you noticed that you have a fallback position – maybe across all relationship situations, *or* with one person in particular like a partner? Make a note of what you do here:

Pledge to yourself not to use a fallback position in your relationships. Instead use an appropriate response to each situation.

Those rose-coloured expectations

One of the most common difficulties people have with their relationships, no matter what area of their life, is overly high expectations. In fact I'd say that overly high expectations can be as damaging to your relationship happiness as having expectations that are too low.

Chloe's unhappy story

Chloe, 39, an artist, had never had a successful romantic relationship. She was the only daughter of two parents who were both doctors. They completely doted on her, and they'd spoilt her with gifts when they weren't around. Chloe had only ever really known one world – and that was where the universe revolved around her. It wasn't that she was a horribly spoilt princess-type in her behaviour to friends and colleagues. But in romantic relationships it was a different story. She had enormous expectations of being the centre of a boyfriend's attention. Chloe expected a boyfriend to 'mind read' and 'know' what kind of romantic surprises would make her happy. And so on.

Some boyfriends lasted longer than others, and it was when her last boyfriend Michael broke off their engagement that Chloe finally realised she had to change. She was heartbroken by the break-up, as well as fearing she'd never have children, considering her age. Michael's parting words were that 'no one could ever fulfil her expectations'.

Chloe's happy beginning

Chloe decided it was time to break free of her unrealistic expectations. After seeking help with this issue she came to understand how such overly high expectations harmed her relationships. She tried the following strategies.

Empathy technique: Chloe put herself in Michael's shoes and tried to imagine the pressures he must have felt in their relationship. She thought about the way he did things, plus the way he felt about things, and imagined his feelings in response to what she was asking. By genuinely trying to think as he did, Chloe realised how difficult he must have found her expectations. The penny dropped when she realised that the anger he expressed during the break-up resulted from feeling inadequate in the face of her demands.

Film script technique: Chloe used the film script technique to bring to life memories from her relationships. She sat back, relaxed, and imagined herself as a cinema-goer, viewing a film of her relationships. She replayed in her mind different experiences and episodes from her relationships. Doing this helped Chloe recognise the emerging theme of her overly high romantic and relationship expectations.

Redress the balance: With these insights, Chloe felt she'd be able to redress the balance of her expectations when she next dated. Chloe decided to challenge any feelings that surfaced when she was dating that told her a man wasn't paying her 'enough' attention. She resolved to examine her expectations, and his behaviour, carefully before she jeopardised any future relationship. Chloe now felt optimistic and much happier, despite the fact that she was still healing from her break-up with Michael.

The 'three Ds'

Other ways relationships can be affected by the 'three Ds' – **damaging**, **destructive** and even **dangerous** beliefs and behaviours:

◆ They can make you emotionally dependent.
◆ They can make you insecure and full of self-doubt.

♦ They can make you seek out unrealistic confirmation of your worth, as in Chloe's experience.
♦ They can make you angry, bitter, hurt, and so on.
♦ They can make you vulnerable to doing things you don't want to do.
♦ They can isolate you from others.
♦ They can sap you of your energy, self-belief, self-respect and confidence.
♦ They can take away your personality, whatever makes you unique.

Developing a cycle of trust

Earlier in *Happy Human* I mentioned the 'cycle of *mistrust*', where, say, you were hurt in the break-up of a relationship and became mistrustful of future potential partners. This mistrust makes establishing a new relationship difficult when relationships are already tricky enough. I'd like you to consider the power that the 'cycle of trust' has to enrich your relationships.

No matter if you've been hurt, scarred, or harbour emotional pain that comes into play in your relationships, the cycle of trust has the power to strengthen you and increase your potential for happiness. There are two elements to growing your cycle of trust:

♦ believing in yourself
♦ daring to take some risk in your relationships.

We discussed self-belief in Chapter Two and it comes into play with the cycle of trust when you have the belief that you'll make the right decisions when you bring people into your life – whether they are friends, partners or colleagues. When you believe you have the ability to judge whether someone will bring happiness or unhappiness into your life, that's when you start trusting. You trust yourself and you trust them. Then by trusting them you take *some risk* that they'll treat you in the way you wish to be treated.

Top tips for trusting

♦ Don't rush trusting someone, but do go with your very important intuition about them. If it flags up any wariness then listen to it and respect it.

♦ Does their behaviour match what they say to you? If from the outset they do as they say, for example they meet you at the time they said they will, or ring you when they're supposed to, that's positive confirmation that they're worthy of this aspect of your trust.

♦ Do they make you feel good around them? If the answer is 'Yes', again that's confirmation that your judgement is correct.

♦ Have you disclosed something personal about yourself to which they reacted with respect? This is confirmation that they're trustworthy with your feelings.

♦ Have they begun to open up to you about personal information? Then they're trying to establish a cycle of trust with you.

Step by step, keep building trust, deepen your relationship and enhance your happiness. You can always take a step back if someone you're getting to know does something to break the cycle of trust. Trust is crucial to your relationship happiness, regardless of the type of relationship. Trust allows you to be yourself and know that you're not going to be ridiculed. It also allows you to relax, let down your guard and allow love into your life – and to love in return.

Your inner child and how you relate to others

I strongly believe that all of us have an 'inner child' that represents our most basic beliefs about how others will treat us, what our 'script' is, and how we relate to others, including the big issues like the love we *want* and the love we're *able to give*. Think of your inner child as right at the core of your personality, feelings, hopes and dreams. It can be helpful for your relationships when you learn to treat your inner child with love and care. The more you love and care for yourself, the more you're able to trust, and to bring worthy people into your life.

You know I think it's important to tap into your creative self so I'd like you to think of your inner child as something precious, fragile and vulnerable that requires care and love to grow into a stronger you. Take a minute to visualise yourself as a young child. What did you look like? What things did you do? Do you remember how you felt about anything like your friends, siblings or parents? Try and create a real picture of this younger self who resides within your heart.

Just as I asked you to coax the little devil that might sit on your shoulder to become a softer, kinder voice within you, so too you need to say to your inner child that no matter how it's been treated (including if you didn't have a happy home-life as a child) you'll treat it better. You'll nurture and love your inner child.

Make a pledge to your inner child not to ignore it and instead to nurture it:

 ....

Part of that nurturing process involves letting those people into your life who are good to you, and setting boundaries around those who cause you hurt or pain *of any type*.

Who do you feel good around?

As you develop happier relationships it's right to ask yourself just who do you feel good around? Who brings out the best in you? Who do you feel secure with, that you can be yourself, warts and all, around? I ask this because some people live under the fallacy that love hurts. Of course we can be hurt when we have a disagreement with someone we love, or go through a break-up, for example. However, love shouldn't hurt in a way that devalues, disrespects and undermines you. I'm sure you know the difference between those people who make you feel good and those who make you feel bad about yourself.

Think through those you've had the happiest times with over the last year. How could you work seeing more of them into your diary? In what ways can you reconnect more frequently? Picking up the phone is always preferable to sending an email or text. The human voice has such power to make us feel emotionally connected. Get some dates with them into your diary now. Let those people who make you feel good share your precious time.

It's not about quantity, it's about quality

You might be saying to yourself right now, 'I don't really know more than one or two people who make me feel good.' It's not quantity that matters! It's the quality of your relationship and how you make each other feel. I know people frequently worry about their life being a popularity contest with others, seeing who has the most friends. When you view friendships and other relationships like that, you lose sight of the importance of simply being around that one person – or those six people – you feel good with.

Confident communication techniques for your relationships

Across your relationships the thing that holds you together is *communication*. Poor communication skills hold you back from enhancing your relationships and your happiness. You can optimise and strengthen your communication in very simple ways. These will help you forge and nurture your relationships.

Use eye contact: We're in such a rush that most of the time we're speaking to someone we have one eye on our mobile and the other eye on some paperwork. Eye contact goes right to the core of our psyche and heightens communication.

Claim responsibility: Claim responsibility for what you're saying by using 'I statements'. With these you begin a sentence about what you want or think with 'I'. For example, you're discussing a relationship issue with your partner – then you'd say, '**I think** if we spent more time at the weekends together we'd feel more connected.' That's more powerful than saying, 'You know, maybe we need to think about our weekend time.'

Be clear: Particularly when talking about a sensitive issue, be clear, and don't beat about the bush with what you're saying. You're far more likely to get crossed wires if you can't get your words out clearly.

Be positive: if you have a difficult or sensitive topic to discuss, highlight something positive around the area before tackling the difficulty.

Practice makes perfect: if you find it hard to express yourself, practise what you want to say. For example, if you want to strike up a friendship with a new colleague by asking them to share lunch with you, or ask someone you're attracted to out for a drink, simply practise it in private. Then you'll feel confident about what you're saying when the time comes.

Active listening: as well as giving eye contact to someone who's speaking to you, reflect back to them what you think they mean. So for example, if they're describing their feelings about something, you can say, 'So you feel that X, Y or Z makes you uncomfortable...' This type of active listening makes the person you're with feel confident that you care about what they're saying.

Gender differences: some men find discussing their feelings difficult at first. It's a good idea to ask what he 'thinks' rather than what he 'feels' about something. A careful choice of words in your conversation will get you a lot further.

Happiness Principle Six

Your relationships with others are crucial to your happiness. Nurture and care for them and expect to be treated as you treat others.

Your relationships have the power to enhance you and your happiness and/or bring you unhappiness. But happiness goes both ways, and you affect those you relate with in a profound way too.

Key elements in maintaining relationships

All relationships need thought, care and maintenance if they are going to be successful and bring you happiness. Try applying the 'key elements' below to your relationships with your partner, family, friends and work colleagues.

Key elements that hold true for all relationships

Establishing boundaries: With any relationship you need to set boundaries. But you might ask what I mean by setting boundaries. In a nutshell, you set boundaries on other people's behaviour if it makes you feel uncomfortable, unhappy, disrespected, or any other negative feeling. You can set your boundaries by:

♦ telling them you don't like their behaviour and you won't tolerate it.

♦ letting them know what you will tolerate: say, a discussion of your differences.

♦ highlighting to them their unacceptable, even poisonous and toxic behaviour.

♦ repeating your message when the situation arises again.

♦ removing yourself from the situation if it calls for it.

It can feel daunting to set your boundaries in this way. Trust me, you have the power within you to do so. You can transform relationships by establishing what you *will* and *won't* tolerate – the earlier the better.

Treat others as you expect to be treated: Just as you might want to stop certain behaviours in others, you need to be aware if you're guilty of damaging behaviour. Always notice when you can sense yourself not playing fair. Listen to others' criticisms of your behaviour and then decide for yourself whether their criticism is justified.

The 'three Rs': You could practically conduct all of your relationships by the 'three Rs' as follows:

♦ You show **respect** for yourself and for your partner. When you have self-respect plus respect for others you'll be aware of hurtful and harmful behaviour from either direction.

♦ You take **responsibility** for your part of the relationship. When you take responsibility for your share of the relationship, then you behave in an emotionally mature way. You do not become dependent on the other person for your happiness, nor do you let them get overly dependent on you. You realise that what you put into your relationship, you're likely to get back.

♦ You are **realistic** about what makes an emotionally healthy and happy relationship.

Embrace these and you'll have healthy and happy relationships.

Accessing love: We all have individual needs when it comes to how much love we need to feel from another person in our life, and/or that we need to be demonstrated towards us. The key here is to learn how to access the love you need from your nearest and dearest.

♦ The first step to accessing love is to learn to give it openly and easily to them. Make sure you tell those close to you – romantic partner or other – how much you appreciate and love them.

♦ The second step is to learn to let them know when you need an extra fuss or a kind word and a hug. The clearest way to do that is to practise short, straightforward phrases like, 'I've had a tough day and I'd appreciate a hug from you.' If you're far apart, access love and comfort on the phone and through emails and text.

Key elements for happy romantic relationships

Harmony and compatibility: When it comes to harmony and compatibility in romantic relationships I've identified five main areas that couples tend to agree or disagree over. These are my five **'F' Factors**. Be aware that these are the five main areas that can bring you and your partner harmony and happiness or disharmony and unhappiness. They require special attention.

1. **Family**: Some find it hard to agree on what part 'family' plays in their lives. Two big problem areas are how much time to spend with each other's families, and whether one person is too involved with their family, for example, the 'mummy's boy' scenario. Setting firm boundaries on overly intrusive family members and sharing out your extra time between your families helps create harmony.

2. **Financial agreement**: Arguments about money feature in around 30 per cent of break-ups. Main problem areas concern how much you spend, and what you spend it on, versus how much you save. It's critical you compromise and plan your finances together.

3. **Fun and leisure**: As mentioned earlier, research shows that ideally couples should share a couple of hobbies as well as having one independent interest. It's important to find the balance that works for you.

4. **Friendship circle**: Many couples find they don't necessarily warm to each other's friends and/or they get envious over how much time their partner spends with others. Striking a balance between spending time with friends you both enjoy, or separately with friends you like as individuals, is the healthy solution.

5. **Fanciability**: In real terms this is the 'f*** factor'! Fancying each other straight off is easy. Where problems begin is when one of you goes off sex or you have different levels of sex drive. Keeping the romance alive and being willing to experiment a little will help keep things lively.

Romantic happiness and health: There are many great reasons to forge a strong relationship and that may well include marriage. When it comes to your health and happiness many studies show positive benefits in a long-term relationship, including one study on blood pressure that found being married led to better health.[27] When it comes to pure happiness and contentment, marriage also looks like a good bet.[28]

Cherish your long-term partner: In the daily grind it's easy to take for granted our most important relationship – the one with our partner. Marital research found that feeling taken for granted was cited by a majority of unhappy couples. It comes down to a combination of treating your partner how you wish to be treated and ensuring that both of you feel you can access love easily from the other. You can create a loving feeling in so many ways, from big demonstrations of love through many small gestures, throughout your daily life. These demonstrate genuine good will and love towards the other person. Remember Victor Hugo's quote, 'Life's greatest happiness is to be convinced *we are loved.*'

Destructive and damaging behaviours in romantic relationships

There are certain behaviours that should ALWAYS be avoided, as they damage happiness with a partner.

Giving the cold shoulder: Research shows that those who fail to resolve quibbles or rows and go to bed in chilling silence are on dangerous ground. Often silence seems the easy way out of a wrangle or a way to cause immediate hurt. Better to say you need time to think through a reply to something than to simply give the cold shoulder to your partner. Don't let cold silences go unchecked. Use a positive tone of voice to generate confidence that you can get over the coldness.

When the celebrations stop: When you stop celebrating anniversaries, birthdays and special events it can be hurtful. These celebrations punctuate daily life and generate warm memories, so ensure you keep enjoying them.

Letting the laughter die: When you no longer laugh together it's easy to allow the daily grind to take over. Life will feel dull and grey and you'll find it hard to remember the last time you two had fun. Ensure you build enjoyable little SPH moments into your relationship, including a proper, weekly or fortnightly 'date' doing something you both enjoy.

Failure to compromise: In the first flush of love you're always compromising because you want to please your new partner. Longer term, many people become more selfish about compromise, damaging relationship happiness. Always discuss finding compromise in straightforward terms. Examine both your expectations – is there an obvious middle ground? If not, take turns over the things that require compromise.

Beware of creeping negativity: This is one of the most destructive behaviours of all. Where once you smiled upon your partner, now you view them with disdain. Where once you listened to their views, now you deride them. Relationship research confirms this behaviour is particularly destructive to love and respect. If this rings a bell, immediately begin reminding yourself daily why you fell in love. Select your partner's three best qualities and visualise them. Think of the nicest thing they did for you recently and hold onto that.

Dig deep and say sorry: Even if you feel you're 'right' about an issue, sometimes it's best to let things go. Also, you can never go wrong by saying you're sorry that something developed into a disagreement. Those simple words can mean a tremendous amount and have a real healing effect.

Put the sparkle of happiness into your relationship

The following are a few small ways you can cast a little sparkle into your relationship:

♦ **The spark of spontaneity**: Spontaneity is terribly important to keeping your relationship alive. I'll be discussing spontaneity in more detail in Chapter Nine. It might feel like a tall order, when you're part of a busy couple, but a little trick is to actually *plan it*. Go through your diary and mark down some dates when you will do something 'spontaneous'.

♦ *A helping of love*: You can lay the table, sit down to dinner and barely speak – or you can put on soft music, light candles, and tell them as they sit down how much you've been thinking of them during the day. Make a point of doing such loving gestures regularly.

♦ *Change is good*: We can become very set in our ways and that can have a bad influence on our relationship happiness. Surprise your partner by getting a new look, booking a new restaurant or suggesting a walk in a beauty spot you've never visited. Little bits of change can put some zip back.

♦ *Do the unexpected for them*: Offer to do something they'd least expect, like sensually washing their hair. Run a candlelit bath, ask them to lie back, and then gently wash it.

♦ *A shrine to your love*: Do something symbolic that celebrates your love. For instance, plant a special bush or buy a pot plant that's your partner's favourite variety. Make the point that it represents your love. We can easily lose sight of what our relationship means and this can become a symbolic focal point for your love.

♦ *Wasted wishing*: Don't waste time wishing your partner would change to be the person you want them to be. Accept them as they are as long as they adhere to certain standards of behaviour, like respectfulness.

♦ *Do them a favour*: You're both busy and so you may fall into the trap of one-upmanship where you bicker along the lines of, 'But I've done more than you today', and, 'Oh no you haven't, my schedule was packed!' Turn off this automatic response and instead do one little chore that benefits them directly.

HAPPY FACT: *One key difference between happy and unhappy people is that happy people spend more time thinking about the good things that happen to them, and unhappy people spend more time thinking about the bad things.*

Key elements for happy friendships

Much research demonstrates how important friendships are to our well-being and happiness.[29] However, I find many people neglect friends the way they might neglect a romantic partner (they shouldn't do that either!). Nurture happy friendships with this handful of hints:

♦ *Have the wisdom to know it's not all about you*. Don't become a friend that only talks about your own issues, problems and dilemmas. Your friends might also need you to lend an ear.

♦ *Give affection and care freely*. If you don't hold back affection and care with your friends then they'll also give more to you.

♦ *Don't just disappear and go off the radar when you're busy*. It only takes a moment to let friends know you've got a busy week, or couple of weeks, ahead at work or with family visiting.

♦ *Don't insist friends take on your battles*. It's tempting when, say, you're breaking up with someone to expect friends to side with you, but that's a selfish sort of friendship that will lead to unhappiness.

♦ *Know that they have space in their heart for more than your friendship*. Don't feel hurt or envious if the friend you care for also has other friends. We all have the capacity to care for more than one friend.

Key elements for happy family relationships

The potential for family members to fall out is staggering. It doesn't have to be that way. You can enjoy happy family relationships by practising the following, as well as applying the advice for friendships above:

- ◆ *Family scripts – what role do you play?* I've mentioned family scripts and it's terribly important to think about the role you've been 'given', how that may cause problems, and how you can solve those problems.

- ◆ *Have the wisdom to accept you won't agree on everything.* You might relegate certain topics to 'no-go areas', accepting that they always cause problems.

- ◆ *Treat family members with the kindness you would show those outside the family.* This means being patient, considerate and watching your tongue.

- ◆ *Being family doesn't mean being the same.* You could take three strangers in a pub and have more in common with them than with your family members. Never forget that and treat each member as an individual. Appreciate their differences and give every family member a chance to shine. Celebrating your differences can be healing; and wouldn't life be boring if we were all the same anyway?

- ◆ *Don't fuel family fires.* Don't get involved in rifts between other family members. Best to let them know you're being neutral and you won't take sides.

- ◆ *Acknowledge any habitual emotional responses your family brings out in you.* You have the power to quell your knee-jerk reactions to family issues.

Key elements for happy work relationships

As you spend about a third of your adult life at work, it's crucial you enjoy happy working relationships. Key elements include:

◆ **Finding a balance between aspirations and fair play.** It's wonderful to aspire to great things but that shouldn't be your sole focus at work. A sense of fair play will give substance to the contributions you make at work.

◆ **Allow yourself to shine.** Many people work hard and do an excellent job, but don't point this out to a busy boss who fails to notice. You can highlight the good work you do without sounding arrogant.

◆ **Thoughtfulness towards others is rewarding in itself.** If you can lend a hand to a colleague in need, or help someone develop a skill, it can be incredibly rewarding and give depth to your experiences at work.

◆ **Work to live, don't live to work.** You might enjoy your work but don't let it overtake your life. Always make time for loved ones.

Loneliness is only human

We've considered how to make relationships happier, but what about when you feel you *lack* relationship connections? Feeling lonely and believing that others around you feel connected to their loved ones can be very difficult. Loneliness is often due to feeling you can't reach out to others, particularly because of worry about being rejected. You'd be surprised how many people would love you to reach out to them!

Not only can loneliness be soul-destroying and cause much unhappiness, but it also has implications for your health. In fact research shows it can be as bad for your health as smoking and obesity.[30] So as well as bringing people into your life to combat lonely feelings, it's good for your health.

A big part of human nature and happiness is wanting to feel connected to others above everything else. Unfortunately, feeling lonely can form part of a bigger vicious cycle. You feel lonely, so you don't feel 'good enough' and assume others will reject you. You give off negative body language, so no one approaches you, and that confirms to you that there's something wrong with you. The cycle continues even when, say, you move to a new job and wonder why you haven't made new friends.

Again I ask you to trust me that many people are in this situation. It takes courage to reach out and change it. The happiness rewards are tremendous when you feel reconnected to others.

Reach out to someone new

Break out of this mentality by making the first move. Keep it simple: suggest a coffee during a break, or a glass of wine after work. Join an evening class and talk to the person next to you. Say 'Yes' when someone invites you to do something after work or after a night class. Be ready with a smile and light banter and soon you'll feel happier connected to others.

The gratification of giving

Part of reaching out also includes *giving*. We can get so wrapped up in ourselves that we forget there are others in more need. So much happiness can be found in what you give to others. It's important to take the focus away from yourself sometimes and shift it to others. Altruistic behaviours are rewarding as well as having the potential to enrich your immediate community. I believe we do less of this nowadays because we often feel disconnected, leaving us with less community spirit.

What kindness have you done for another person lately, that was simply about doing good for someone else?

Just think what a difference it would make to human happiness if everyone did a small kindness, every day, for someone else.

Do something for your immediate community or a charity

There are many ways you can give a little care or skills to your immediate community, or on a bigger scale in terms of charitable work. Trying to be kinder to yourself is important in building more happiness, but psychological research also shows that giving to others is good for all concerned.[31]

In fact you might have felt that sometimes your attitude is too much about 'me, me, me'. It's easy to get wrapped up in yourself; now might be a good time, in trying to create happier relationships in your life, to also look outwards to the needs of others. Lend a hand in local community schemes as many are stretched for resources. Local schools also need governors or other volunteers. Or explore volunteering for local or national charities. To make a genuine commitment, think through how your skills or life experiences can benefit others. It might only be a small gesture, and perhaps only once every couple of months, but you can make a difference, even in little ways. The personal happiness that comes from helping others or improving your community is rewarding.

I firmly believe that in any human relationship, to give is to receive – you receive contentment, fulfilment and happiness simply by giving.

I've covered many important points about enhancing your relationships. I hope you embrace at least a few of these and that leads to more happiness. Fear can hold us back from relating to others – and fear is what we're now going to look at in other contexts.

Build Your Happiness Habit

Spread the love, and every day let someone you know you care about them.

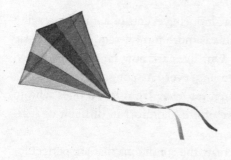

7

Don't Fear Your Fears

*Happier the person that takes one step forward
into the unknown than stands still with fear.*
Ancient Chinese Wisdom

Throughout *Happy Human* I've highlighted powerful emotions influencing our happiness. Now we need to look at another powerful emotion that can diminish your life in many ways, including your experience of happiness. This emotion is fear. Humans developed fear as a powerful warning that they needed to act immediately and *fight* the danger, or *take flight* from it. But as we've evolved, so too has our environment. This means we still have this capacity for fear but often it gets channelled in negative and destructive ways.

Think about the lives of ancient men and women: in a sense their fear was more 'pure'. By that I mean it was easily under-stood in terms of their survival – they faced fierce animals, fearsome intruders and fear-inducing events of nature like raging storms. Because their fear was more pure it required that basic 'fight or flight' response. Our lives are now far more complex. They're fast-paced, demanding, ever-changing, and we live in a disconnected fashion, often far away from loved ones who in times gone by would have offered comfort in difficult or fear-inducing times.

Our modern lifestyles create the conditions that are perfect for producing fear in us, but in a way that isn't so easily understood. It's not so 'pure' a fear to worry about how you're going to meet deadlines when your computer system has crashed, and you have no idea how to fix it, plus you can't reach your computer consultant. The natural human 'fight or flight' reaction doesn't really provide a solution to such modern dilemmas.

There still exist age-old fears of the unknown that often translate nowadays into generalised anxiety. And there are also age-old fears of creatures and creepy-crawlies in the shape of what we call phobias. But I firmly believe modern life sets up many fear-inducing situations that aren't easily overcome – there isn't a clear path to solving them, and so they feel overwhelming, and research confirms this.

Some critical types of fear

There are many different types of fear and I'd go so far as to say that fear is at the root of most human unhappiness. Think back to some of the stories I've highlighted throughout *Happy Human* – fear is at the heart of them, like Deborah's fear that she'd never be good enough to find a partner (you may recall she blamed her parents for that), and in Chapter Nine we will read about Stephen's fear of his boss ringing him, probably to criticise him.

First I'd like to touch briefly on four types of fear and their definite influence on your happiness.

1. ***Generalised, non-specific worry and anxiety***: when you feel a pervasive sense of worry, foreboding, dread and fear that doesn't necessarily relate to one specific thing. It can be specific – like only being attached to work issues – but usually it underlies most of your life. What sets it apart from specific, non-phobic fears (below) is that you find it hard to pinpoint exactly what you fear. If this persists it can become generalised anxiety disorder (GAD), which affects about 3 to 4 per cent of the population.

2. ***Phobic-type fears***: when you have an irrational fear of something like non-poisonous spiders. We don't live in a country populated by deadly creepy-crawlies, yet 20 per cent of us fear spiders.[32] Or you could be afraid of something like heights or flying. These fears are irrational because the feared things are actually harmless, or you'll never come into contact with them, or they're statistically very unlikely to be a problem. For example, those who fear flying often happily get into a car, although they have 100 times more chance of having a car crash than a plane crash.

3. ***Specific, non-phobic fears***: these are fears where there's an identifiable reason for the fear. Say, you have a new boss who's a bully and unpredictable, so it's quite rational to fear what they're going to do.

4. ***General fearfulness***: where you tend to have a fearful, timid nature and it's part of your personality to feel anxious about life generally.

Do you recognise your feelings in any of these fears?

All of these fears have the potential to make you unhappy. No one escapes fear of some type and at some point. Just as with harbouring emotional pain, which is hopefully acknowledged and healed at some point, fear is part of being human. You can take action to free yourself from any type of fear (strategies to come).

Your fear can negatively impact your life in these ways:

◆ It stops you in your tracks
◆ It holds you back from your potential
◆ It prevents you having new experiences
◆ It drains you emotionally – as do all such negative emotions
◆ It prevents you getting what you want in relationships
◆ It stops you setting boundaries on unacceptable behaviour
◆ It halts your creative juices
◆ It means you don't seek recognition when you deserve it
◆ It kills your natural curiosity
◆ It stops you living your life in so many ways

Why do we succumb to our fears rather than facing them?

As mentioned, our natural 'flight or fight' response doesn't protect us in modern life because many people feel trapped by the way they live. They have nowhere to 'flee' – for example, they feel there's no escaping mobiles, email and BlackBerries. People feel obliged to keep them on 24/7. We're also not supposed to 'fight', so a pistols-at-dawn scenario with your over-demanding manager wouldn't happen.

This leaves many feeling helpless. That's when fears that were once faced or fled from override people's ability to cope, and they panic.

Where else does happiness-quashing fear come from?

Apart from the way we live today there are two distinct sources for any fear you have. What's called 'intergenerational social transmission' of fear is largely responsible for phobic-type fears, as well as for having a fearful nature. This is where the fears of your parents are handed down to you as a child, staying with you unless you decide to change that.

The other main source of fears comes from life events that are painful, traumatic and damaging. Let's say you're in a serious car accident. Recuperation is slow and difficult, and not only do you develop a fear of being in another crash but you also start to develop generalised fears of coping with life. You can see how any such event can become a negative cycle.

The ironic thing about many people who develop fears *of any type* is that they're regarded as strong, and at least quietly confident, types. Unfortunately many such people allow things to pile on top of them until, like the straw that breaks the camel's back, something finally elicits fearful feelings, even panic, in them.

 How much does fear hold you back?

Answer these three key questions to determine whether fear might cause you unhappiness:

1. Does fear of *anything* – be it your boss, or a fear of dogs, or something else – stop you from doing *anything* like expressing yourself, going out, feeling happy?

      Yes   No

2. Do *fearful-type feelings* like anxiety, worry and/or foreboding play on your mind, making you uneasy or unhappy *to any extent*?

      Yes   No

3. Do you honestly feel that part of your personality could be described as 'fearful'?

      Yes   No

Your responses
Any 'Yes' answers at all means that fear and/or fearful feelings impact on your life negatively and they will eventually, if they haven't already, cause you unhappiness. This unhappiness *is unnecessary.*

Cloud-lifting moments –
when we face fear

You might think, 'Why should I face my fear? It doesn't affect me *that much* after all.' I hear this refrain from fearful people, just as I hear it from people who have an emotional hole or wound that they think can never be healed. The reason you should face your fears is that people who have done this (including myself) find it a revelation; they feel a burden lifted from their shoulders, and they suddenly see the world with a more open and optimistic outlook. They also realise what they've been missing out on – that while they were locked into their fear, they missed out on life.

Free yourself from your fears

Let's take action now: face your fears, and free yourself from them. Once fearful feelings and subsequent fear responses start, if you don't make relevant changes to overcome them, they continue. Let's look at some general points first, that impact on fearful feelings. Improving any of these areas will increase your levels of happiness:

♦ *General time management*: are you always time-short? Start saying 'No' to extra responsibilities and worry less about getting further ahead at work. Instead enjoy a better quality of life, with fewer fearful feelings.

♦ *Work and family commitments and responsibilities*: the more these eat into your time, the more fearful feelings will increase. Explore with your manager how to streamline work and be more efficient. At home, delegate chores and let go of any perfectionist tendencies.

♦ *Your relationships*: as we have just discussed relationships in the last chapter, you know how important it is to nurture them. They serve as a protective factor against fear.

♦ *Overall health*: if you're eating on the run, drinking to relieve stress, smoking and not exercising, such things will exacerbate feelings of fear.

♦ *Leisure time*: just as loving relationships improve your inner strength, well-being and ability to face fearful feelings, so too does taking time to enjoy a book, a walk, a film, and so on.

♦ *Relaxation and breathing techniques*: as feelings of fear often involve many physical symptoms, it's important to learn to relax major muscle groups and breathe in a controlled fashion. Practise daily sitting still, warm and comfortably. In turn, tense and then relax every major muscle group from your lower legs, thighs, stomach, back and neck, down your arms. Meditate on your breathing, making it measured and relaxed.

A courageous letter

This technique can be very helpful. Write a letter to yourself about *your bravery* and why you're worthy of a life that is not over-shadowed by fear. Make a note of a time when you faced something difficult and didn't back down. Include how you have the inner strength, self-love and love from others to face anything. Write it as if it's from yourself *to yourself*. Or as if it's from someone that cares very much about you. Think about what they'd tell you and write it out in detail. Keep it close to reflect on when you feel fear rising up.

Avoid your fear – avoid life!

Avoidance is a big issue for people in fear. People start to avoid whatever they're frightened of – a neighbour's dog, a conversation with a partner over a difficult behaviour, or a bullying colleague. Avoidance is easy – but not satisfying! You can find all sorts of ways to avoid what you fear.

But avoidance means that life and happiness is slowly chipped away. The more you avoid, the smaller your world becomes, the fewer chances for happiness. And avoidance never solves anything because you aren't facing what you fear, and finding a solution for it – like learning that most dogs don't bite, that you can talk to your partner about something difficult without being rejected, and you can let your colleague know you won't put up with bullying.

Specific steps for phobias as well as other fears

Looking at the following treatment for phobias will show you how very practical tactics can help you face your fear one step at a time. These steps for phobias can also give you ideas for facing any fearful situation in a practical way. I emphasise 'practical' because phobias and fearful responses make us so emotional – and irrational – that solutions need to take the emotional sting out of them.

I'll use the example of facing a very common phobia – dental phobia – for a step-by-step approach. You can substitute your particular fear in the following steps, tailoring the steps to your situation.

Before any step remember to relax your breathing and ease body tension, otherwise these heighten the physical feelings associated with fear.

Set aside a two-week period where each day you can allow yourself 20 minutes to spend tackling your fear or phobia with daily tasks. Two weeks is the minimum time frame, and when you think about how this may profoundly enhance your happiness, it's well worth the effort.

Seven steps to facing a fear

1. Draw up a list, starting with the *least* frightening thing involving your fear, up to the *most* feared task. For dental phobia, the least feared thing might be walking past the dental surgery with a friend – and the most would be getting a full dental check. Praise yourself for each task completed and get family and friends to encourage you too.

2. Now, with a friend or family member, walk past your local dental surgery, practising relaxing your muscles and breathing regularly.

3. Then do this two or three more times until you can walk past the surgery on your own without panicking or crossing the road. This may take a few days.

4. Next ring the surgery and explain to them you're trying to overcome your fear. Ask if it would be OK if you came and sat in their surgery to get used to it. Most surgeries are happy to help.

5. Then go and sit quietly in the waiting room while you overcome any tension by relaxing and breathing regularly. Listen to the sounds and get used to the smells of the surgery. If it's the sound of the drill that bothers you, record the drill noise and play it somewhere you feel comfortable, like your kitchen. You'll get used to it.

6. Next make an appointment to meet and chat to the dentist. Explain to the receptionist that this is an appointment without treatment. Most will accommodate you. Keep your breathing regular and relax those big muscle groups as you sit for a few minutes.

7. Your final task will be to go for a check-up. Again keep your breathing regular and relax those big muscle groups throughout the check-up.

At any point if you feel fearful or panicky, share this, letting a friend or the dentist know – that will ease your burden.

Signs and symptoms of a panic attack

When you fear something, and have felt helpless in the face of it, you may experience a panic attack. This can happen even when you've been avoiding something you fear, because even if you physically avoid it, you still harbour that fear within you wherever you go. Symptoms of a panic attack include a tightening sensation across the chest, shortness of breath, palpitations of the heart, feeling dizzy, having sweaty palms and a dry mouth, shaking, general anxiety and finding it hard to think clearly. In an extreme panic attack you may feel detached from reality or disorientated.

You should see your GP about any such symptoms to discover if they're caused by panic. During an attack use this **Five Point Panic Plan**:

1. Remove yourself from any crowded conditions.
2. Sit down if at all possible and steady yourself.
3. Regain control of your breathing by inhaling slowly to the count of five and exhaling slowly to the count of five.
4. Sip water slowly (carry a water bottle with you).
5. Distract yourself, for example, phone a friend or think about something unrelated to your day like a calming holiday memory.

Once you've overcome your attack you need to explore what's at the root of your panic and face your fears, as outlined in the seven steps above.

HAPPY FACT: *The term 'epicurean' associated with pleasure-seeking is derived from the Greek philosopher Epicurus. However Epicurus had a much more realistic approach to happiness, focusing on fulfilling your basic needs, including your connection to others, rather than simply pleasure-seeking.*

Will yourself to courage

In Chapter One, and elsewhere, I mentioned the power of your will. Perhaps your will can make an incredible difference in no other area as much as facing your fear. Think of your will as like a cheering audience at a sports match, the theatre or a concert. The people in that cheering audience want you to succeed. They *will* you to succeed. Now that you love and respect yourself (I hope you've taken on board Happiness Principle Two), you'll have the self-belief to know that you can live with courage and without fear. We humans are powerful beings with an amazing capacity to change and redirect emotional energy into positive things.

Worry – the runaway enemy

One offshoot of unchecked fear is worry. Worry is only a small word, but believe me it has large consequences. It takes you away from self-belief and leads you step by step into self-doubt. Eventually it runs away with all your positive energy. I've worked with people who literally worry their lives away.

♦ *A key fact about worry*: it doesn't get you anywhere.
♦ *A key fact about action*: it gets you everywhere. So take action over your worry. Treat it like the enemy. As with any aspect of fear, face what causes you to worry, and do your best to solve it.

Happiness Principle Two

You can become fearless. It's within your power.
At some point in your life you became fearful,
but you weren't born that way.

Ultimately you can free yourself from fear – you don't
have to live a life of fear, anxiety and worry; instead
you can face changing circumstances, difficulties and
hurdles with courage.

Embrace change and
increase happiness

I'd now like to highlight a significant area of your life where fear plays a truly negative role that *you may not even realise*: it's the fear and anxiety that stops you from *embracing change* in its many forms. Many people feel so stressed in the way we live today as well as feeling compelled to cling to habitual patterns of behaviour (to be discussed in Chapter Nine). They also feel bombarded with a certain type of change through the daily demands of their workplace, principally through technology. So to gain consistency in their life in the face of all such demands, they avoid change when it comes their way in various forms.

What form does change take?

I really am talking about all the types of change that people reject – both the little things like being able to 'seize moments' but turning these down, and the bigger things like rejecting larger opportunities for change. From the 'drop in the ocean' things of life to the meaningful, change is avoided and rejected. Why?

Fearful feelings, and/or feeling overwhelmed, mean you all too often *close down* from change. People who fear change even in the smallest way decrease their chances for a happy experience. They also miss out on the confidence-building that goes with doing something different and new.

Specifically, change can range from getting a new hairstyle, to deciding to change your job; from changing the place you have lunch, to changing the way you relate to a loved one. Change can come as an offer to learn a new skill at work, to a friend suggesting you come to an evening class with them. Change can be offered in an opportunity to travel abroad, or to find a new flatmate. Change can be daunting, exhilarating, and all points in between. The value of change is immeasurable and when we embrace it, it can rejuvenate us, challenge us, get our creative juices flowing, be a simple pleasure, or even be a negative or unpleasant experience – but we can learn from that.

When did you last say 'No' to change?
What change were you faced with, what did someone suggest that meant change to your plans, and so on, that you decided you wouldn't embrace?

 ....

Why else do people fail to seize the moment, take opportunities and embrace change?

I find there are two core reasons, apart from feeling under pressure, why people fear change.

♦ First there are those who stick rigidly and neurotically to a routine, and can't let go and seize the moment. They avoid change because of the unknown. They can't control the unknown so they'll *keep control of what they know.*

♦ Then there are those who avoid change because of the *fear of failure.* They don't go for a new job opportunity, even though there's a job on offer they'd dearly love, because they might not get the job and so would 'fail' in their own eyes. They don't approach the person they find attractive because they think their offer of a drink might get rejected and so again they would feel that they've 'failed'.

Whether it's wanting to stay in control or fear of failure, such beliefs hold you back. They also make human experience that much more difficult, because every human being experiences a great deal of change. Those who resist change essentially resist life and happiness.

Here's a second completely truthful quote that I couldn't resist for this chapter: 'Paralysed with fear, I watched my life pass me by.' (Anon)

Make a pledge to yourself

◆ Don't let life pass you by.
◆ Grab opportunities with both hands.
◆ Risk *not* being in control of something different or new that you decide to try.
◆ Embrace change with gusto.
◆ View crossroads and transition points in your life as great chances to grasp new things.
◆ Say 'Yes' the next time someone offers you the chance to do something different.
◆ Be curious, not daunted, by things that are different from your normal routine.

The dangers of 'what ifs'

When you resist change, you risk living a life of 'what ifs'. That's because, ironically, when people don't seize moments and/or take opportunities they often end up plagued with 'what ifs'. Much unhappiness stems from those who end up living life as a series of 'what ifs'. '*What if* I'd done this?' and '*What if* I'd tried that?' and so on. They feel unhappiness because they're left wondering if they've missed out on something, if life could have been better if they'd taken an opportunity, if they might have had a happy connection to someone if they seized the moment to go out with them, and so on.

Have you experienced a 'what if'? Make a note of what it was about:

Seizing the moment can be life-changing, happiness-enhancing, and exhilarating – so grab those opportunities with both hands!

Life is a roller coaster

When it comes to our potential to develop fears, worries, and anxieties by being presented with things that feel out of our control, with possible change, new opportunities, and all such things, it becomes obvious that even the most blessed life is like a roller coaster. And although as I've repeatedly said, we have the will and power to shape our behaviour, our responses and choices, we still do a bit of a 'dance with destiny' when it comes to the array of things we're presented with and their impact on us. But this should make life exciting, not frightening!

One powerful idea that has come from 12-step programmes for addiction – and that is relevant here – is to learn to recognise those things that are in your control and those things that aren't. With that wisdom you can face what you can go with, control, and/or enjoy or learn, and you can also face what happens with those things that are out of your control. They don't have to damage you or cause you unhappiness. Accepting when things aren't in our control, and knowing when to let go of things outside of our control, is a powerful and ongoing lesson of life. Life can't be leashed in like a pet, there's a dynamic quality that should be embraced.

The 'silver lining' choice

When life throws you those things that bring on fearful feelings, or threaten your control, or even upset or hurt you, there's always the 'silver lining' choice. This is not seeing something as a failure, but learning to identify the best in a bad or unhappy situation. Have you learnt from something that didn't go to plan? Meditate on what you could get from that experience. You can always choose to learn something, and I see that as the 'silver lining' choice.

Gaining confidence, shedding fears

Whether you face something that makes you feel fear or anxiety, or that daunts you with its potential for change, you can become your own Confidence Coach. Here are some tips, tricks and techniques to do this:

- Try 'feelgood' tricks like singing your own anthem (a song you love and that lifts you up) or visualising a happy memory when feeling fearful.
- Remind yourself of a recent time when you rolled with some change and perhaps something good came out of it.
- Remind yourself of any 'what if' moments you've had and how you don't want to experience such moments of regret again.
- Develop a new interest or skill that will help create a new frame of mind. Think through it step by step – what do you need to do to achieve this? Make a 'to do' list. For example, research local colleges for evening classes. Make a decision about which is best, how to apply, and so on. Using manageable steps you'll reach your goal, building confidence.
- Accept that failure is fine. If you've tried something new and it didn't work, you're not a failure! You had the confidence to put yourself out there. At least you've learnt something.
- Become a warrior – you can face things that daunt you and grab them with both hands, or you can roll over and quit.

♦ Telephone the person who always makes you feel good and tell them this. We often hide sentimental feelings but telling people good things boosts our confidence to relate better to others. It makes us emotionally stronger and more able to face the world.

♦ Find your inner spirit to face change by *seeking it out*.

♦ Finally, I've personally found useful, learn to relax in the face of changing circumstances. Pause and take a moment to reflect about what good can come from them.

You should be ready for anything life throws at you now. Let's turn our attention to something very powerful within you but that most of us neglect – that's the power of our intuition and how it affects our well-being and happiness.

Build Your Happiness Habit

Do one thing differently today to challenge any fear of change and to boost your confidence generally, making you less fearful.

The Power of Your Intuition

We all live with the objective of being happy;
our lives are all different and yet the same.

Anne Frank

There is a powerful part of our human nature that I believe is, on the whole, deeply neglected in our modern lives: that is our intuition. I say 'on the whole' because only a minority of the people I meet are in touch with their intuition, and really believe in its power. We were given our intuition – our sixth sense – for a purpose and yet we have all but abandoned our natural intuition in the way we now live. I call our intuition our sixth sense because it is over and above the other five senses we almost completely rely on – hearing, seeing, touching, smelling and taste.

A starting point for understanding our intuition, or our sixth sense, comes from a school of thought in psychology, Gestalt psychology. One of its core concepts was an idea that can help us to think about ourselves, as humans, in a holistic way. This idea, or concept, is that when you consider the function of a whole, complicated system like a human being, then you need to consider the 'whole' as greater than the sum total of its parts.

What does this mean, that the 'whole' is greater than the sum total of its parts? If you were to take each of our five classic senses independently, they each tell us something about the situation. So you might be able to *see,* through your sense of sight, from your partner's expression that they're unhappy with you. Or from what they're saying you can *hear,* through your sense of hearing, an unhappy or angry tone in their voice. Each one of our five senses provides us with lots of information.

To understand your intuition, I'd like you to think of all five of those classic senses coming together. What they give you – a huge, whole package of information – is even greater than each one individually. Think of this as your sixth sense. Your intuition is like all of these aspects working together, giving you a wealth of information about a situation, another person, and about your own feelings, and responses to these at an overall level.

Your intuition is particularly good at gauging what's really going on in a situation, or with someone else, when they're not giving you all the information that you can actually 'sense'. You actually know more is going on underneath the surface than is being said. Think about when I mentioned body language in Chapter Four in relation to how it can make you look miserable, and so a colleague wouldn't approach you. When you can gauge someone's mood, say, without them even specifically telling you how they're feeling, how do you think you do that? Because you can make these judgements over and above what they specifically say. From someone's body language, plus perhaps what they say as well, your mind sifts through loads of signals that form an overall picture and comes up with an answer or conclusion.

How does this ability affect your happiness? It affects your happiness in so many ways that it's incalculable. Let's say you're single and you're out at an event thinking that tonight may be your lucky night. You spot someone across the room, and although consciously you know you're attracted to them, you also start to assess all sorts of signs and signals coming from them. These signs and signals give you much more information and allow you to come to a conclusion that they'd respond *positively* if you smiled at them. It's not one single sign or signal that helps you reach that conclusion. Instead it's your dynamic assessment of the whole situation, at many different levels – through your sixth sense, your intuition. And this assessment occurs very rapidly.

Once you've reached the conclusion that someone might be interested in you, even though they're across the room and you two haven't spoken, it puts a lift in your step and a smile on your face, and that in turn gives them something to respond to. Their intuition starts picking up what you're signalling. So the cycle continues.

Obviously it's not just in the signs of attraction that our intuition is there helping us assess situations. It occurs across all situations, and understanding and using your intuition can heighten your experiences and interactions from the bedroom to the board room and all points in between.

Why did our intuition develop?

When you think about our development as human beings you can come to understand why our intuition evolved in the first place. It evolved because it provided an excellent source of information that many believe helped guide our most basic instincts of survival and reproduction of the species. And our survival and reproduction are two important things!

Let's think about the survival of our ancient ancestors. They needed to be able to understand sometimes imperceptible signs from a situation or another person and make quick judgements about how to respond. It's important to remember that ancient humans were continually encountering new situations that they didn't have any previous experience of. Many of these situations would be potentially life-threatening. For instance, they came to 'know' that when the hairs stood up on the back of their neck they needed to be aware that they faced some sort of threat. Signals like that helped them to realise that there was something greater happening in their environment than simply what they could see or hear. So their intuition evolved to help guide them through unusual situations, or when they encountered strangers.

Likewise when it came to the importance of the survival of the species – sex – ancient men and women needed to ensure the species continued. This was long before people met up for coffee dates or dinner to start getting to know each other. And also it was long before they'd developed a sophisticated language as we now have, and so ancient men and women had to 'guess' about things like whether a potential mate was fertile, and who would be a good mate to ensure healthy offspring that were also looked after. As they roamed the countryside their developing intuition meant that the early humans became very good at judging who was receptive to sexual advances and who would be a good mate over an extended period of child-rearing. They honed their ability to judge their 'hunch' that someone was attractive – and equally attracted back to them. All of this was essential for their survival, and ultimately the development of intuition still benefits us in our modern lives. Or at least it benefits those who use their intuition, as unfortunately many ignore it.

Risk your happiness if you ignore your hunches

Having mentioned 'hunches' makes me think about how often we ignore little feelings about a person or a situation. Yes, we've all known someone (including ourselves) who with 20/20 hindsight says they 'had a hunch about this or that happening'. But on the whole I think we can be either quite lazy about acting on our hunches or overly sceptical of them. Until, as I just mentioned, after the fact, when we say that we'd had a hunch about something and then it happened. Looking back retrospectively, though, is very different from actually *acting* on a hunch in the first place.

A fascinating piece of research found that our so-called hunches are often based on memories lying just below the surface of our consciousness.[33] As such our hunches have a real basis – because they are based on memories – so we should feel encouraged to act on them more frequently. This study found that we have what they called *untapped intuition* that's based on these unconscious memories of things we've absorbed but have since forgotten. However the memories can then partially resurrect themselves in the form of intuition when we then go on to have a feeling about something – our hunch. But what do we do, so often? We all too often question our hunch when it may well be based on these unconscious memories.

How do our hunches relate to happiness?

When we start to believe our hunches, or at least decide we'll test them before we act on them, we raise our level of self-belief. It's a positive cycle where we have a hunch, we then decide to believe our hunch, next we act on it, then we find that we were right, and finally we get a lift from that enhanced self-belief. This cycle helps us confirm to ourselves that we have this power. This power is about a deeper insight from within us, and that's an exciting thing to possess.

I'm sure you can think of many instances where your happiness would have been affected by acting on a hunch. I clearly remember once, when I was single, having a hunch that someone who worked in an associated department to the one I worked in fancied me. Because I was still suffering a bit from my divorce I decided *not* to take a chance and flirt with him just in case I was rejected. Who wants to act on a hunch that might just turn out to be my own 'fantasy' of him fancying me? How embarrassing would that have been, particularly when I was feeling vulnerable!

So I continued with my work and ignored my hunch. I never treated him any differently from my other colleagues, despite feeling that there was a mutual attraction. Eventually he started dating someone else, and it was only after that time that someone told me that he'd been 'hanging around for a few months hoping to get my attention before he gave up on me'. I could have kicked myself for ignoring my hunch. I naturally then wondered about things like if we would have enjoyed dating each other, if we would have fallen in love, and all that sort of stuff. But it was far too late and I'd missed that moment of potential happiness.

Make a note here of a hunch you've ignored:

✎ ....

What was the outcome? For example, was the hunch confirmed, as in my example? Did that mean you missed out on something?

✎ ....

Intuition is not chance or fate

Let me clarify now that your intuition or sixth sense is not related to the chance or fate mentioned in Chapter Three. Remember, those who believe in chance or fate see it as some power that's outside themself. They believe they are 'buffeted' by the hand of fate or are at the mercy of chance. Intuition, on the other hand, comes from within you. Think of it as the fruition of all your five senses working together, creating a greater source of power.

 Are you likely to use your intuition?

Let's explore how likely you are to use your intuition. Answer this quiz to determine to what extent you use it or ignore it. Select the answer that best matches your experience.

1. Do you ever make a decision based on your gut instinct?

   Ⓐ No, I wouldn't – I need all the facts to make a decision
   Ⓑ I might, depending on the situation
   Ⓒ Yes, I'm very likely to

2. Have you ever 'felt' you knew something but didn't quite know why?

   Ⓐ Not really, I haven't experienced that
   Ⓑ I think I've felt like that
   Ⓒ Yes, definitely, I've had powerful feelings like that

3. Have you ever 'felt' something about someone or a situation but discarded that feeling only to find out later it was true?

   Ⓐ I can't think when that's happened
   Ⓑ Yes, I have done this
   Ⓒ I'm very unlikely to discard such a feeling

4. Do you believe in the power of your intuition to give you important information?

Ⓐ Up until now I haven't
Ⓑ I've considered it
Ⓒ Yes, definitely

5. How do you feel when someone says that they've used their intuition to make a decision?

Ⓐ Very sceptical that they've done the right thing
Ⓑ I think maybe they'll have done the right thing
Ⓒ I think they're wise to do so

Your responses

Three or more 'A' answers

Non-intuitive. You either ignore and neglect your natural intuition or are sceptical that it actually matters. It does matter! Evolution over hundreds of thousands of years has given us this gift. Think of it as a natural power within you that has gone untapped up until now. It's lain dormant within you. It's time to awaken it, or at least be more open-minded about its existence. Try the intuition-building exercises below. You might be surprised how as you learn to believe in yourself more – and that's essentially what believing in your intuition is – you'll enjoy more happiness.

Three or more 'B' answers

Semi-intuitive. Though you're not sceptical about your intuition, you do tend to ignore it. It's partly that sometimes you can feel a hunch growing within you and you might pay attention to it, and other times you don't notice it, or question it. It would definitely benefit you to seize hold of it and use your intuitive power to its full extent. Do try the exercises below.

Three or more 'C' answers

Pro-intuitive. You're undoubtedly in touch with your intuition, or sixth sense. You see it as a positive force in your life and something that is like an extra tool in your box of life-enhancing skills. I wouldn't be surprised if you've tested its accuracy by going with a hunch and then checking with the outcome to see if it matched your hunch. You can undoubtedly see the benefits to your happiness of believing in your intuition as giving depth to your self-belief.

Enhance the Power of Your Intuition

As our intuition is sorely under-used, I've devised some exercises to help you increase yours. I think it's regrettable that we've become a generation that doesn't believe in our gut instincts. And I firmly believe that we miss out on so much because of this – including missing out on much happiness. Think about my example! From experience of working with people I've found that when they doubt themselves if they have a 'feeling' about something, looking for actual proof or evidence of it instead, they can lose out in certain circumstances. It's a reality of life that in many cases you simply can't gather actual evidence or proof of something. For example, in the unhappy circumstances where you have a 'feeling' that your partner's having an affair – I have found that in 99 per cent of cases where someone has a feeling like that they end up being proved right. Sadly they often wait for a number of weeks or months more, living under a cloud of suspicion, before they act on their hunch. It's only the rare few who have an issue with jealousy and become overprotective of a partner, believing they 'must' be having an affair when they're not.

As with any aspect of your personal self – like developing more confidence or self-awareness – you can develop your intuition. I think it's particularly helpful if you go with my view that it's the sum total of all your senses working together. That in turn creates something greater than each individual sense alone. Here are some unique exercises to help you improve your intuition:

Mind reading: To develop some intuitive mind-reading skills you can practise this with a partner or close friend. Obviously I usually recommend straightforward communication techniques with a partner or colleague, and so on, when you want to make a point about something or discuss an issue. And I always say not to expect a partner to be able to read your mind, for example if you're hoping they'll 'guess' something that you're thinking because you don't really want to raise a sensitive topic. However it can give your intuitive powers a fantastic boost to try some experimentation. Try this first with those that you are close to, then you can expand your experimentation to include trying it with other people. This is what you do: when in someone's company, try *relaxing* your thoughts and being *open* to theirs. Forget what's been zooming through *your* mind – you know the dozens of thoughts we can be inundated with, within a few moments. Try focusing on their thoughts and trying to 'see' their inner person. When allowing yourself to clear your mind you allow your intuition to pick up whether they're feeling tense, reluctant, shy, and so on. You can then actually comment on what you've picked up and say something like, 'It seems like you're tense'. I'm sure you find on the whole they'll appreciate that you picked up on their inner thoughts. In fact they may be touched by you intuiting something about them that they haven't actually expressed. That will make them feel a little glow of happiness because they sense that you care about what's really going on with them. In turn this will give you increased happiness.

The timepiece trick: This can be a great developmental experience for your intuition but it can also be beneficial to your life in so many other ways, particularly if you happen to be an over-achiever who gets stressed – if you are, you should try this at least once a week. For a few hours, remove your watch and cover your office or kitchen clock. Now let your intuition take charge of your timekeeping and guide you over how much time has passed since, say, your lunch break. What you'll find surprising is how quickly your intuition taps into your natural body clock. We never give our intuition the chance to show us that it's actually a very good judge of the passing of time. As you get better at this, try going a whole day without a timepiece of any sort.

The power of connected breathing: This is a good technique to try with a romantic partner when you're sitting, lying down, or cuddling. What you do is to let go of your own physical energy and allow your breathing to start matching theirs. As your breathing becomes connected to theirs you'll be surprised how you connect to what they're thinking and feeling. When your breathing is in synchrony it allows your intuition to kick in to the sort of things they're feeling. This can be a powerful way of connecting to them. It's uplifting and creates a sense of well-being. I particularly recommend it for partners who don't have much time together and where one or both may feel quite lonely, say, during the week if they have to be apart. This sort of intuitive connectedness can be very healing to something like loneliness. And I think it can benefit practically any partnership. It might also benefit your partner's intuition if they allow themselves to go with the flow of your breathing. This is similar to a Tantric breathing technique that helps you achieve mutual orgasm. And how much happiness could *that* bring you?

Intuitive touch: If you have a partner or even a close friend or family member that you'd feel comfortable massaging, then a powerful way to develop your intuition is through touch. But this massage would be given in a different way from how you might normally give a massage. You might give your partner a sensual massage or give a family member a friendly massage to ease a tense back. To develop intuitive touch you need to free your mind of any thoughts and allow yourself to 'feel' through your fingertips the stresses and strains in your loved one's muscles as you massage them. Get in synch with their breathing, too, along the lines of the exercise above. By doing this you allow yourself the opportunity to absorb their emotional state. This in turn allows your intuition to get in touch with their state of mind. Again this can have benefits for your well-being, for their well-being, and connecting you both in a positive way.

Free association: This next intuitive development exercise also taps into your creativity. Take a few moments and relax your mind, banishing all thoughts from it. Once you are relaxed I want you to look at this simple line drawing:

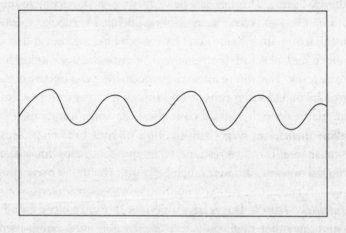

While you look at it, try 'free associating' a few different images from it. For example, you might see this simple image as rolling waves. See what you come up with when allowed this freedom. Such creative exercises, which free your inner mind, also boost your intuition to see beyond what's actually there. In other words, to 'see' more than the sum total of the parts of the rectangular shape with the bisecting line.

Guessing game: This exercise is very helpful in developing your intuition with a partner, family member or best friend. What you need to do is for both of you to get comfortable and sit back to back. Make sure that as much as possible of your hips, back and the backs of your heads are touching. Then reach around and clasp hands or link elbows. It's important that you agree to be silent and simply try to 'sense' what they're feeling. Take a few minutes, relaxing in this position, to absorb this. Ask yourself if they're feeling relaxed, tense, or happy in this position? After a few minutes tell each other what you think the other was feeling and/or thinking. This can be an illuminating exercise where both of your intuitive powers can be increased. It is also a trust-building exercise for those close to you. Earlier in *Happy Human* I mentioned the 'cycle of mistrust' – a few moments spent in this exercise can help restore a sense of trust if it's been damaged for some reason, or strengthen trust that's already there.

Your intuitive gift: Use any opportunity where you need to exchange gifts – like on an anniversary or at Christmas – and suggest you both choose a 'symbolic' gift that means something special. Then make sure you use your imagination and creativity in choosing something unique. As you mull over choices, bring to mind the image of the person you are buying for. See if you're drawn to any particular choice. The hunch your intuition gives you may well be based on unconscious memories (remember that research mentioned above) of something they've said in the past about wanting a particular item. Then when you exchange gifts, take a few moments to appreciate what message they're trying to give through the choice of their present. Guessing the symbolism behind the gift will stimulate your intuition – both of you should try that. Again, this sort of exercise can strengthen your bonds and increase your well-being, in turn increasing your levels of happiness. Also think about this in terms of spontaneous gift-giving. There's nothing like a little surprise gift to bring some extra happiness to your partner or close friend. But again, take a moment and bring them to mind, to get intuitive stimulation for your choice of gift.

Sensory deprivation: This is a brilliant technique to use to help sift through conflicting thoughts and allow your intuition, or sixth sense, to come to you. Use this when you're in a quandary or dilemma about a situation or about what someone's thinking or feeling. Try some 'sensory deprivation' to stimulate your intuition. This is almost like the opposite of what you're doing when using all of your senses together to give you a more profound picture of what's going on with something. What you need to do is darken your room, and turn off anything like the radio, TV and your mobile. Next lie quietly for a few minutes. Relax your breathing and clear your mind so that the only scenario you're aware of is your immediate surroundings. Without the distraction of your other senses (like hearing and sight), now you can try to get a feel for what your intuition is trying to tell you about your quandary or dilemma. Let that scenario come into your mind now. While your other senses are 'deprived', is this allowing your sixth sense to come forward and give you guidance? You may well find it does.

Hopefully with this development of your intuitive power you will also develop more self-belief when it comes to facing quandaries and dilemmas. Again, in turn that will increase your sense of well-being and happiness over making a decision.

Streamline your thinking zone: Now let's think about where you actually do your thinking, and/or your relating, and/or your work. What's this area (your office, your sitting room, and so on) like? Is it cluttered and chaotic? Believe me, from my work as a life coach I know that the more distractions there are to your intuition, the less intuitive you'll be. With that in mind, now's the perfect time to streamline important areas in your life. You can tackle places like your office, your sitting room and your bedroom when it comes to your relationship, and so on, one at a time.

Keep a note: Using your sixth sense is particularly good for gauging someone's mood and you'll soon know if you're getting better at doing this. This can range from your boss, who you're considering asking for a rise, to someone you've just met and you can't tell if they're attracted to you. When you have a gut feeling, or hunch, that your boss *will* be responsive to your request, or that special someone *will* be receptive to a smile, that's the perfect time to test yourself. Go for it *at that moment* and keep a note of how many times your intuition is correct about a situation. A fascinating piece of research found, you should be right at least 70 per cent of the time.[34] Hopefully you'll get an increasingly higher hit-rate as you learn to go with your intuition when it 'speaks to you' rather than holding back and doubting yourself.

At this point you might really start to feel the power of your intuition and hopefully experience the reality of a deeper self-belief from developing this skill.

Happiness Principle Eight

When you develop and embrace the power of your intuition, you deepen your self-belief, which in turn brings you more happiness.

Belief in your intuition is ultimately a belief in your deepest self that embraces all of your senses. When you attain that level of self-belief you develop a greater understanding of the world around you and your life. That means you can enhance those things that make you happy.

Jennifer's unhappy story

How would you feel if your intuition or hunch about someone told you that you *should* be concerned about them – but when you confronted them they looked you in the eye and replied with a boldfaced lie? It would feel pretty awful that your gut feeling told you one thing yet they denied it. This is what Jennifer had to contend with.

Jennifer, 38, an events organiser, had a hunch that something was wrong with her husband, David, 41, a surveyor. He'd become somewhat secretive about certain things – or at least, 'secretive' was the only way she could describe it. She asked him why he was late, or why he locked his study door some evenings, and the answers he came up with just didn't ring true. She had this feeling right in her heart that he was fibbing, but she'd back off quickly when he protested that *she* was a bit paranoid.

This feeling increased for Jennifer when their internet savings account balance dwindled unexpectedly. They'd been saving for some home improvements and needed to dip into that savings account to meet their monthly bills. That was when Jennifer first noticed their dwindling balance. When Jennifer suggested that they sit down and go through their incomings and outgoings to work out where their finances stood, and asked David why he'd withdrawn money from their savings account, David virtually panicked. She'd never seen him like that and wondered what on earth was going on. To cut a long story short, after a number of days where Jennifer couldn't even get her hands on their current account statements because David had supposedly 'lost' them, David finally confessed that he'd been gambling on horses and had sustained large losses. He had raided the savings account to cover some of these losses.

This confession came like a bolt out of the blue and Jennifer was completely floored. Jennifer had no idea that he had any interest in gambling, let alone on horses. She felt utterly betrayed and also angry that every time she'd asked him what was going on – because her intuition told her that things weren't right – he had denied anything was wrong, and had wasted so many opportunities to confess his gambling addiction to her. Most of all she felt terribly unhappy that everything they'd based their marriage on – mutual respect, love and trust – seemed to have been tossed to the wind by his behaviour. Where once she'd felt happiness and contentment in her personal life, now Jennifer was unhappy and sceptical. She wasn't sure if ultimately she could forgive him and trust him again, but she was prepared to work at it.

Jennifer's happy beginning

Rebuilding relationship trust: When trust is broken, the most critical first step to rebuilding it is to make a commitment to *doing as you say you'll do*. In other words your behaviour has to match your words, or – obviously – the person who has broken the trust has to match their behaviour to their words. When trust is broken it's usually because of the opposite – that what someone has said to you is *not* what they're actually doing. Jennifer and David's trust urgently needed to be rebuilt and part of that was David committing to go to Gamblers Anonymous (GA). He started going to two meetings a week during this crisis phase. He also committed to telling Jennifer when he was feeling confident about his gambling impulses and when he was feeling weak. She felt this was particularly helpful as she really wanted to know the truth, even if the truth could be testing. It might cause her some anxiety to know that he had just had a wave of impulses to gamble, but that's far less anxiety-provoking than if he kept her completely in the dark about his innermost feelings. David would ring her if he was at work and feeling vulnerable, and they'd chat this through. He eventually got a sponsor at GA who also served as a 'crisis buddy' that he could contact outside of GA meetings when he felt vulnerable.

Rebuilding self-trust: Jennifer realised that her intuition, or sixth sense, had been right all along – there had been something wrong with David's behaviour. But she hadn't trusted herself enough to keep pushing her fears and instead would relent quite easily and believe what he had to say. Now, though, she needed to re-establish trust in her intuition. She did this by making a point of going with her gut feeling whenever she had a decision to make, which in her line of work as an events organiser she had to do frequently. These decisions and judgements included anything from meeting a new client and judging whether what they saidabout their 'maximum' budget was true, to being there at the end result of her work – an event – and judging the reactions to it and how honest people were. Jennifer made a note of her gut reaction and then acted on it. Then after the fact she'd double-check and confirm if her gut reaction and intuition were correct or not. In other words she kept a note, as I recommended you try in my last intuitive development exercise, above. Jennifer found they were spot on and pledged to listen to her intuition from that day onwards. She also practised a number of my intuitive development exercises.

These two major advances on their levels of trust gave Jennifer the impetus to stand by David. They both felt happier at this point about the progress they'd made since the 'crisis day' when David had revealed all. Jennifer and David also committed to do a number of relationship-boosting exercises, which are really the topic of another book focusing on relationships.

Your spirituality and happiness

I know that for many people their spirituality is important to their happiness. And for many, their spirituality is intuitive. They have a 'feeling' in their heart, and even their gut, that it's important to them and adds much to their life – almost in the way that our intuition adds to our other senses, heightening our experience of our world. Let me clarify that when I say 'spirituality', I include a whole range of people, from those who believe in a traditional religion, to those who may be 'humanist' in nature and believe in the power we have as humans to do good, respect others, and bring understanding and love into the world. And of course all of those who fall between these two points.

In this sense I see your spirituality, if you feel you have that aspect to your life, as again vastly different to any belief in fate and chance. Yes, there might be overlap between having spiritual beliefs and believing that part of these beliefs is about 'fate'. But on the whole I see the choice to *embrace* some sort of spirituality as very different to giving up your life – and your power – to something outside of it, like fate and chance.

I only want to touch on this because I don't want you to feel I've excluded your spirituality if this is an important part of your life. I completely recognise how it may be bound up with your well-being and how much happiness you experience. In fact a number of studies have shown that those who have a spiritual or religious belief system in some ways experience more happiness. One study found that those who have a strong faith and regularly go to church experience a sort of buffer against stress, and report greater life satisfaction and well-being than those who do not.[35] What this research found was that a strong religious belief system seemed to act as a sort of assurance against the uncertainties of life. Part of this well-being may link into the comfort believers receive if they belong to a religion where there's a belief in the afterlife. But also this research found that, as believers, they gained comfort simply in the here and now from their belief system.

I find such research very interesting, especially considering that I consider myself to be a happy human, and a spiritual person, but certainly not in a traditional religious way. I come from much more of a humanist background and like to believe in the inherent good of mankind and the ability of good to prevail. I can certainly understand the benefits of my belief system in helping to bring happiness into my life. I certainly don't subscribe to the view that you have to be spiritual or religious to be happy. However, I've met many people – and know there are many more – who feel very lost in our modern world, emotionally unconnected and impoverished. They have a longing for something, but don't believe in religion, yet they don't know what will make them feel connected in a meaningful way to their world. They may find that developing some sort of feelings of spirituality benefits them, as research suggests. I strongly believe that developing their intuition, and recognising the power we have in ourselves, can be one step in the right direction to contentment and happiness.

 HAPPY FACT: *The American Declaration of Independence of 1776 cites 'the pursuit of happiness' as an important goal for every single person.*

The healing side of intuition

I definitely want you to consider the potential healing side of developing your intuition. Some intriguing research has found that those who were diagnosed as depressed, and were then allowed to swim and snorkel over a two-week period with dolphins, gained lasting benefits with alleviation of their depression.[36] Their well-being was increased over at least a three-month period. Patients reported that they found, in some intuitive way, they made an emotional connection with the dolphins. The research did point out that part of the benefits that patients had might be partly due to having felt out of touch with nature. Swimming regularly with the dolphins reconnected them to nature. But also part of the

202 How to be a Happy Human

benefits came from the sense that they were communing at an almost inexplicable – or intuitive – level with nature.

This is a wonderful outcome to consider. Not only does it give us an important message about being in touch with nature, but also underlines the power of our intuition to *let us be in touch* with nature. In developing your intuition about your life, about others in your life, and the situations you encounter, it seems you may also raise your ability to feel connected to nature generally. Make sure you use this new-found intuitive force to help connect you to our wonderful world. I mentioned previously in Smaller Picture Happiness the importance of doing something simple, like walking through a park, and allowing yourself to enjoy the moment. These moments should be part of your everyday life.

Your happiness 'aura'

I'd like you to think about your aura – that special, intangible 'something' about you that others recognise and pick up on, largely through their intuition. How can you develop a happy aura that gives off positive energy and a sense of well-being?

Here are the key things to think about:

- *your body language* – is it welcoming or defensive?
- *your facial expression* – is it warm and calm or is it stressed?
- *the things you say* – are they kind and nurturing or are they critical and hurtful?
- *the things you think* – are they calming and inspiring or negative and destructive?

With those four things in mind, really take the opportunity to think about the aura you present to others. Can you identify potential sources of negativity in it? Maybe you'd accept that often your body language is less than welcoming. Or perhaps some of the things you catch yourself saying are quite critical to others and it would benefit them and you to use a gentler voice. From time to time revisit these thoughts about your happiness aura. Because there is one certainty about your aura – the way people 'see' you and the feeling they get from you is then fed back to you. This is one of those dynamic loops where something can bounce back and forth between people, including the general feeling they get when they are with you.

The childish side of intuition

There are many lessons we can learn from children, and one in particular is about listening to our intuition. Children have astonishingly high levels of intuition that are often ignored by the adults around them. How many instances can you think of where a child has blurted something out that might have been a touch embarrassing, but was actually true? Over the years I'm sure you've witnessed many such events where 'out of the mouths of babes' often come difficult truths. I can think of one such event just recently when I was at a social gathering. A young boy who was there with his mother, amongst this fairly large group, ended up saying rather loudly that he 'didn't like' a particular man, even though this boy hadn't had any more interaction with this man than witnessing his mother saying hello and exchanging a few minutes of social niceties with him. I know for a fact that particular man has a large ego and he's not a very warm person! That child's mother tried to hush him quickly, which was of course the right thing to do considering the circumstances. But it's fascinating to think how this child's intuition picked up on this man's negative vibe, or aura.

We can learn something from this truth about children and their intuition. And in the example I used of this little boy, we'd learn to be aware of those people that we immediately sense are a bit toxic. Or even if we couldn't stay away from them because, say, they're a work colleague, we wouldn't let them poison the way we feel about ourselves. Unfortunately, over the years we often get our intuition knocked out of us, or at least relegated to a very low position in our consciousness. Instead we should be nurturing the wisdom from our 'inner child', as I mentioned in Chapter Six.

I hope you're now actively thinking about your intuition – your sixth sense – and how you can put it to work for you in your life and to help you embrace more happiness. It's a power to be reckoned with, and if listened to, it can help guide you and your choices. Harness it and believe in it!

It's time now that we think about you and your habits. You'll be surprised to find just how much of your life is one great, big, long habit – and how much you can change and improve it when you break the habits that bring you unhappiness.

Build Your Happiness Habit

The next time you have a hunch about something, act on it immediately. Use it as a test of your intuition and decide on the basis of what happened whether your hunch was right, partly right, or maybe even wrong. In the latter case your intuition definitely needs more outings!

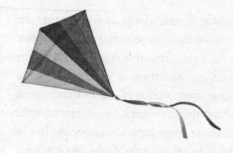

Humans are Creatures of Habit – Happy and Unhappy Ones

> *When one door of happiness closes, another*
> *opens; but often we look so long at the closed*
> *door that we do not see the one which has*
> *been opened for us.*
>
> Helen Keller

If you were with me now, sitting down and chatting, and I asked you to describe to me *exactly* what your waking-up and morning routine was this morning, I bet I could predict with 100 per cent accuracy what it would be like tomorrow. It would be *exactly* the same, down to the smallest detail. It might only change at the weekend or on holiday. And even then it might stay pretty much the same.

Let's dip into an imaginary waking-up routine: you undoubtedly pull back the bedcovers in exactly the same way, put the same foot down onto the floor first, followed by the other, pick up your dressing gown and slip it on in exactly the same way as every other morning. Next you walk to the bathroom along the very same path you always tread, switch on the light and blink into the mirror. Once there you do everything in the same order – from splashing water on your face, to running a brush through your hair, and applying your make-up if you're a woman.

Your stomach begins to rumble and it's time for breakfast. I'd lay good money on the fact that it'll be the same breakfast as the day before. You switch on the kitchen light and continue your morning routine in the same order, to every last detail, as you did the day before – and the day before that. Whether it's a rushed cup of black coffee, or a deftly prepared full breakfast of toast, cereal and tea, I'm absolutely certain the thing that you do first, next and afterwards will be the same. I'm sure you could do it all blindfolded and half asleep – in fact you probably are half asleep as you do most of your morning routine.

Think about it: *am I right*? Do you actually do everything exactly the same from the moment you wake up until the moment you leave your front door to face the world?

How can my prediction be so accurate? It's accurate because as humans, we are absolute creatures of habit and routine. Our habits and little routines give structure and backbone to the rest of our life. They serve a purpose to help guide us through life with a sense of security that all is 'OK' and 'the same' in what sometimes can feel a rather threatening and stressful world. Nothing's too surprising, and we can count on the way we do things to take us from rising, to going to bed last thing at night. We even habitually sleep in the same position, with the same window open, and the bedcovers pulled 'just so' over the part of our body that we like covered. It's all one long series of habits.

The crystallisation of our habits

From the moment we're born our habits are dictated to us by our parents and their routines. Our habits soon become 'crystallised', meaning that we don't even have to think about them. They are second nature to us. And because of this, once crystallised, they move out of our conscious awareness into our unconscious mind. Maybe you haven't considered it before, but it's your unconscious mind that guides you out of bed through your bathroom and breakfast routine. Take a young adult who has flown the nest and look at their 'new' routine, and it will resemble the routine they had in their parents' home to an uncanny degree. Though admittedly, everyone knows what it's like when you have to move house, begin a new job, even start a new relationship, and suddenly you have to adapt and tinker with your old habits to fit them into the new situation or environment. You have to consciously think about where you're now going to put everything in a new home or on your new desk. You need to consciously consider where your bed is in location to the new bathroom and how that part of your routine will work in your new home. But as soon as you've adapted your old habits to the new situation, they become crystallised very quickly and we once again act on them unconsciously.

Our habits and day-to-day routines can definitely affect our levels of happiness. They can impinge on our happiness in a variety of ways as we shall see in this chapter. An awareness of your own habits and how they positively and negatively affect your life can be eye-opening in small ways. but in much bigger ways too.

The good, the bad and
the ugly habits

Of course there are many good – or positive – sides to habits. Mostly they save us a great deal of time and energy. We'd hate to waste time thinking about, say, what we should do first when we hop into the shower every morning. There's no point in debating with yourself whether to shampoo your hair first, or wash your body first, or to ponder whether to scrub your face before either of those, each morning. To have such debates about every aspect of our daily routine would be quite frankly soul-destroying! Also, the fact that our nearest and dearest know what our habits consist of means that they can often guess or judge when and what our next move will be when it comes to something like our daily routine. They streamline their habits alongside ours so that on the whole we end up working well together. It's the same with colleagues who get to know our little habits and routines and can judge whether it's, say, a good time to try and grab five minutes with us to go over a report, or whether we'll be having our habitual 'elevenses'.

Our habits mean that we can go from A to B quite smoothly and expend the least energy possible worrying about things. Because our reserves of energy are terribly important to our well-being, habits mean that we don't deplete these reserves for any unnecessary reason. So you can confidently think of your daily habits, *on the whole*, as time- and energy-saving rituals and routines that keep your life flowing as it should.

I'm sure you can feel a 'but' coming along at this point, and you'd be right. The problem is that our habits can also sometimes become negative or bad habits. They can become negative – or our responses to them can become negative – in many different ways, but here's a simple example: if you allow 30 minutes for your journey to work because habit tells you that 30 minutes gives you three or four minutes' leeway for your bus being late, then that's pretty much all well and good. However, when an accident means your bus is 25 minutes late and so your routine is thrown out of kilter and you're going to be 20 minutes late for a meeting, how do you respond? Do you respond calmly and figure there's nothing you can do about it? Do you ring a colleague and ask them to greet the person who's showing up in your office for a meeting and make them a cup of coffee? That'd be great. Or do you get upset, feel stressed, your chest tightens, you curse under your breath, and then go on to allow this hiccup to your day to cast a shadow over your morning? It's important to understand that we have habitual ways of responding when our habits and routines get interrupted. And these habitual ways of responding can be either positive or negative.

But there are other reasons why habits can be 'bad', including things like:

- they become too time-consuming
- you become such a creature of habit that you live by a very rigid routine
- you find it very hard to let go of habits when you must face a new situation
- you believe that your habits form the basis of 'good' routines and try to impose them on a new partner that comes into your life
- you missed out on seizing spontaneous moments because you're locked in to your habits and routines (you may recall I mentioned the importance of seizing moments in Chapter Seven)
- they come to cause you, or others, some sort of discomfort or upset.

All of these *potential* negative outcomes will impact on your well-being and your happiness levels.

Let's take the 'classic' problem where a woman spends a long time on her grooming routine. How long you spend on your routine is your business, but be warned that such routines might have a negative impact on other areas of your life. I've worked with many women (and their make-up routine was *not* what they consulted me for, but happened to arise in various conversations about why, say, they had arguments with their partners) whose make-up routines severely cut into their day because of the preparation time they required for getting ready to go to work. These routines also caused arguments with partners when they took too long getting ready to go out for an evening. Before you accuse me of sexism, yes, of course there are men who spend longer in the bathroom than their partners, but in my experience this is less common. It's one thing for a woman to insist that she needs to spend an hour doing her hair and make-up, but it's another matter when her partner is standing around waiting as they grow increasingly late for a dinner reservation. Or when she, herself, starts to feel stressed because there just aren't enough minutes in the day to squeeze in a morning make-up routine and an evening one, too.

It is just these sorts of stresses and strains caused by our habits and routines that can actually profoundly affect relationships or other aspects of our life. What about the common complaint of, say, a family of four who all share one bathroom, and Dad insists on sitting on the toilet for 20 minutes each day reading the paper? This is another common yet crucial source of arguments, all due to his toilet habits. He feels he has a right to his daily 'habit', whereas the rest of the family begins to think he's a selfish pig! His daily habit causes stress within the family, arguments and family members leaving home for the day in a huff. I've known cases of such habits being the tipping point, or the straw that broke the proverbial camel's back, when a relationship breaks down. Very often it's a person's annoying, inconsiderate and bad habits that are cited when someone breaks up with a partner. Such an outcome obviously has profound effects on your happiness.

Habits can also become worse than 'bad' – they can become downright ugly. A perfect example that springs to mind is the cigarette habit. It's a very ugly habit for the smoker, and those who have to inhale their passive smoke. You can't argue it's anything but ugly when a habit can kill you. I've met families who have lost a loved one to the cancer caused by cigarette smoking, and unhappy families they become indeed. They can't understand why the person they loved couldn't give up their cigarette habit. They feel pain, complicated by feelings of anger and hurt from their loved one's behaviour that ultimately left them bereaved.

But when I think of 'bad' and 'ugly' habits, a whole other type of habits springs to mind – and these are 'emotional' habits.

Practical and emotional habits

It's quite helpful to break down our habits and routines into those that are practical and those that are emotional. I have already highlighted the most practical types of habits of all – those that get us up in the morning, streamline our daily routine, and help get us to bed. Our other habits, which form the backbone of the rest of our day, such as how we go about our working day, the way we do our shopping, our cleaning, and all those sorts of activities, also fall into the practical category.

I wouldn't be surprised if you're wondering what I mean by 'emotional habits'. I've actually already touched very briefly upon them when I asked how you'd respond to your morning travel routine being disrupted by an accident that made your bus late. That's when we start getting into the domain of emotional habits. We, as humans, have habitual types of emotional responses to things. These habitual responses, again, can be positive or negative. They can enhance your interaction with the world, your relationships, and so on, or they can diminish your interactions with the world.

These habitual ways we have of doing things that fall into this emotional category occur in many ways. Let's say you're in a relationship where one of your emotional habits is to always reach out to your partner and give them some physical affection when they have a problem. You simply stroke their arm or give them a brief hug to calm them down. This becomes a habit because of your previous experience of these situations. You've found that your partner gets emotional relief from any stressful feelings from a little bit of physical contact. That contact reassures them and gives them emotional strength. But that contact becomes a habit for you. You'll automatically reach out to them that way when you can sense or know that they're stressed. And that's an example of a positive emotional habit. Unconsciously you know they get reassurance from you, when you make these little physically affectionate actions. This then goes on to bond you two together emotionally at some level and increases your happiness, too.

You might also have certain knee-jerk reactions that become negative emotional habits. Let's imagine that your partner has fairly regularly let you down by being late. (Being late could be a negative, *practical* habit of theirs where they simply don't allow themselves enough time to get from A to B. Or, interestingly, it could be a negative emotional habit that they use to control you in a passive-aggressive way.) Increasingly your automatic reaction, the minute they walk in the door, is to fling down what you're doing and challenge them with, 'So you're at it again, always late, you just don't care!' You don't even wait to hear if they have an excuse. This becomes habitual and even if they did have a good excuse (think of the delayed bus example above, and they got delayed due to an accident) you *react* before you hear it.

Stephen's experience

Stephen, 28, an accountant at a large firm, described how he'd had a difficult relationship with his manager over an 18-month period. It got to the point that whenever Stephen's phone rang, and he could see it was his manager ringing, he got an immediate sick feeling in the pit of his stomach. It was a mix of anxiety and dread. The unfortunate thing was that he'd allow this negative emotional response to become a habit when sometimes his manager wasn't even ringing to criticise his work. Stephen simply couldn't shake it off until the day that he had a complete employment assessment with his manager and they managed to iron out some of their difficulties. This helped increase Stephen's confidence about his work and after that point he learned to prevent this habitual negative emotional response from whipping up in him when he saw that it was his manager ringing him.

If you've ever developed a response like that you'll know how deeply unpleasant it is. You'll also know that it's a waste of your emotional energy and a negative habit that diminishes your well-being. Unfortunately such responses and behaviours can become negative, emotional habits quite quickly – and *without us even realising it* until it's too late and the response has been laid down.

Take a moment to think about your habitual behaviour. Does either of these examples (Stephen's reaction to his manager or your partner always being late) ring a bell with you? These examples may not specifically apply to you but the sorts of feelings and responses they arouse may do. So perhaps you don't habitually respond negatively like that with a boss or a partner. But it could be that you have habitual responses towards a colleague, a child, a friend or family member along these lines. Make a note here about any negative emotional responses that you make and that have become, or are fast becoming, a habitual way of responding:

Now make a note of whether this behaviour is limited to one person, or a specific situation, or whether it cuts across a number of situations or people:

I'd be amazed – and even impressed – if you can't think of an example of a negative emotional habit of yours. I know I've had to break such habitual ways of responding in the past. I'd hazard a guess that if you can't think of this type of habit in your own repertoire of behaviours, maybe you simply haven't identified it yet. It's something to consider and it's positively a good thing to identify and break this kind of habit, particularly as such habits can have a negative impact on your well-being and happiness as well as on those around you. Some interesting research found that it takes three weeks to develop a 'happier' response when trying to prevent negative thoughts and responses.[37] At first glance you might think, 'Crikey, three weeks is a heck of a long time just to change a little response of mine!' Just think how long you might have been habitually responding in a negative, knee-jerk way to certain circumstances. It may have been years – and so three weeks isn't such a long time to develop a new, positive type of response that ultimately gives you a happier outcome.

 A hard habit to break

Answer this quiz to help you identify whether you have unhappy, habitual ways of responding or habits that need breaking or changing in some way. Here's that 'honesty reminder' again: think honestly about your habits, and your habitual behaviours and responses, before answering each question.

1. Do you regularly swear something like 'I won't react like that again!' over a particular behavioural response of yours – and yet break that pledge?

       Yes   No

2. Do you feel bogged down by the routine of your life?

       Yes   No

3. Do any of your habits dominate your life in a negative way?

       Yes   No

4. Has anyone ever told you that you need to let go of some of your 'ways'?

       Yes   No

5. When you think about your daily routine, do things ever feel dull and slightly boring?

       Yes   No

6. Have you ever kicked yourself for 'jumping the gun' and responding in a certain way that turned out to be the wrong or inappropriate response to the situation?

       Yes   No

7. Has any part of your routine or habitual behaviour ever caused disagreements or arguments with anyone?

       Yes   No

8. When thinking about your habitual routines at home or at work, do you ever get annoyed with others for disrupting it?

        Yes   No

Your responses

One or two 'Yes' answers

Happy habits. Based on your answers you undoubtedly feel that you don't get yourself into trouble with habitual patterns of responses, particularly negative ones. That's a positive starting point when it comes to identifying any negative habits – practical and/or emotional – that can creep up on us. So far yours don't appear to have caused you conflict with other people. However if you've selected even one 'Yes' answer, depending on how it affects your life, it may have consequences for your happiness. The best solution is to take a preventative view so that this habit doesn't bring you into conflict with others in future. With that in mind take a look at the suggestions below.

Three or four 'Yes' answers

Some unhappy habits. Although your habitual ways of responding may not yet have caused large amounts of conflict in your life, they certainly have the potential to do so. It's important that you identify where, from your answers, you may be experiencing problems and unhappiness. Try the suggestions below.

Five or more 'Yes' answers

Unhappy habits. I'm sure that reading this chapter has rung some bells for you. The fact that you selected so many 'Yes' answers suggests that you have a real problem with habitual responses – probably both practical and emotional ones – and need to take action to change the way you respond in various situations with various people. Try implementing the suggestions below.

Establishing Happier Habits

***Meaning what you say – take action on the things you say*:** If you regularly find yourself saying things like, 'I swear I'm not going to react like that again', then begin a *chain of actions* that can make sure you stick to those words.

◆ Write down what it is you swear you're not going to do. If you were Stephen you'd write down something like: 'When the phone rings and it's my manager I'm going to immediately put up a big "stop sign" to any negative emotions entering my mind. These will prevent habitual emotional responses like dread and fear from building in me.'

◆ Now you can post that 'memo to yourself' where you'll see it regularly – at the side of your desk or by your phone, for example.

◆ Next you can consider a substitute reaction. Make it wildly different to your normal reaction. Perhaps you can force yourself to think of a funny scenario and actually chuckle (even silently in your own mind, if you're somewhere public like your office). Eliciting an opposite emotional response can combat your negative emotional response.

◆ Finally, think of the solution to that thing that sets off your habitual negative response. As Stephen did, perhaps you need to thrash something out with the person that you respond negatively to.

Tackle self-destructive habits: When you find you are 'kicking yourself' over some sort of habitual response, explore why you're in that situation. Let's say that you're habitually late for meetings. Then, as you arrive late, you 'beat yourself up' as you swing that door open to greet the person waiting for you. You then keep kicking yourself, even after the meeting is over, with your regrets over being late, for the next couple of hours – or even the rest of the day. Ask yourself what it is about being on time that you simply don't manage to do? Believe me, this is a good example to use, as being habitually late is a big issue for many people. This habitual behaviour eats away at their interactions with others and definitely has consequences for their happiness. Sometimes the simple answer is laziness. This sort of habitually lazy response to planning a journey, planning to have a report ready on time, and so on, means the person thinks they'll get away with it and can't be bothered to put the effort into organising themselves. It's only when they're late for the wrong person (for example, their future mother-in-law or their boss) or the wrong event (for example, they miss a flight or are late for a job interview) that they realise they need to change their habits. Of course there could be a more complicated explanation for why someone is habitually late. But it needs to be tackled so that it doesn't become a self-destructive habit. Change yours before it gets to that point! Once you've explored the reasons behind any self-destructive, negative habits, you can then take the logical steps to tackle them. When it comes to the example of someone who is habitually late because they're lazy, they need to implement timekeeping alerts on their mobile or PC, and they need to give themselves stricter deadlines for preparing work, and so on, and they need to plan anything like journey times better.

Let it go: A big aspect of habitual, negative responses or habits is the conflict they bring you into with others. When you find yourself in conflict, for example with a new partner that you've just moved in with, and your morning routines conflict, try letting it go. Challenge yourself and ask whether your habits or routines are really so essential that you must do them without any change. See if you can let some of your routine or habitual responses go. Analyse what happens – does your relationship or situation improve? If so, in what way does it? Letting go like this probably just spreads a little love and your relationship becomes happier. Definitely remind yourself of any positive change on a daily basis.

Check your impulses: Most people can sense a knee-jerk, habitual response coming on. There's an impulse to open your mouth and say what you normally say, or do what you normally do, in particular circumstances. You might recall the 'five-second pause' technique from Chapter Four on Smaller and Bigger Picture Happiness. You can use that to check your impulses. Pause for a count of five before you say or do anything.

Try another way: Commit to breaking negative habits that cause conflict in your life by trying another way. Let's say your new partner has suggestions for altering your morning or evening routine, or anything else that affects both of your lives. Go for it – try out their suggestion. You may find it makes things go more smoothly, or whatever it is actually works for both of you.

Cheryl's unhappy story

What is it like when you *realise* that you're behaving in a way that is damaging to you, your relationships and your life and happiness? Yet you feel a bit helpless to change, despite having this knowledge, because the way you're acting comes from a long-standing habit?

It can feel like a fairly hopeless situation, when actually it doesn't have to be that way. This is what Cheryl, 36, a fashion buyer, found when she finally had to face facts that her habit of flying off the handle when annoyed or a bit stressed was jeopardising her relationship and her career. Not only had Cheryl achieved a great deal in her professional life and now had a great reputation in the business (a reputation that was likely to diminish if she didn't change!), but in her personal life her boyfriend of two years, Andrew, had just moved in with her and they'd started to talk about marriage. Problems loomed in the shape of the drip, drip, drip effect of Cheryl's lightning-quick habitual responses to certain situations.

Andrew, 35, a graphic designer, had a fairly relaxed approach to life compared to Cheryl's hyper-achieving attitude. This relaxed approach showed itself in a variety of ways, particularly when it came to making plans. Cheryl wanted everything in their diary, at the earliest possible time, and for plans to be executed with precision. Whereas Andrew sometimes wanted to change plans if something more interesting came up for them to do. A good example of this would be that Andrew would ring Cheryl at work and ask if she wanted to change such and such a plan. The minute Cheryl got wind that he was about to ask to change something in their diary she'd spew forth something like, 'Oh, for f***'s sake, why can't we just stick to our plans? You know I'm too busy to even think about changing anything!' She didn't even want to listen to his suggested change, as she simply didn't want to have to deal with altering something that had already been put in the diary.

The same sort of reactions meant that Cheryl had become increasingly unpopular with her junior colleagues. She'd snap the minute one suggested that they looked at a different part of a fashion range, or considered buying some items that hadn't been on Cheryl's main list for a particular client. Junior colleagues attempted to tread a careful path around Cheryl for fear of getting one of her lightning-quick responses. As the office environment became more tense, a direct colleague of Cheryl's pulled her aside for a discussion about the younger staff members and how she could manage them better. Cheryl had to admit she was aware of this problem at work and at home with Andrew. Things were tense and strained in the office and in their relationship and she knew something had to change.

When Cheryl discussed the details of what happened she could perfectly describe the almost instantaneous rage that she felt when she'd lash out with her tongue. She admitted how surprised she was that she quickly became calm again. She also admitted to feeling guilty about her bad behaviour once the moment had passed. Again this is a classic post-response feeling that many people report – they almost can't believe how quickly a response comes, and then how quickly it subsides, and they feel calm again. In my experience, people who notice this response in themselves on further exploration actually have issues around stress, anger and even rage about certain aspects of their life. These bigger issues seep out into their habitual responses, tainting them with a certain explosive quality.

Cheryl's happy beginning

Lifestyle evaluation. The first step for Cheryl was examining what was going on in her life generally before looking at changing her smaller, but influential, negative emotional habits. I say 'influential' because, as I mentioned earlier, there can be a drip, drip effect where small habits become the last straw that break the camel's back. Cheryl evaluated the priorities in her life and also the balance of the time she spent at work and enjoying the rest of her life. Cheryl kept a week-long diary of six key elements:

- O the amount of time she spent at work
- O the split between enjoyment and lack of enjoyment during that time at work
- O the amount of time she spent in basic routines
- O the negatives and positives she could determine from her routines
- O the amount of time she spent with Andrew
- O and again the split between enjoyment and lack of enjoyment during that time together.

Identifying patterns. When she'd kept this diary for a week, she then looked for any pattern to her enjoyment and lack of enjoyment, as well as positives and negatives in her habitual routines. The most clear-cut pattern Cheryl identified was that as the week went on, she increasingly responded negatively to Andrew or junior colleagues. This was undoubtedly due to fatigue building up over the week, which ate at her reserves of patience and her ability to keep a civil tongue.

Changing established patterns. The other clear-cut pattern that Cheryl identified was that her life was definitely skewed towards long working hours – something she already realised, but seeing it on paper made it stand out more. She took immediate steps to let colleagues know that they could no longer rely on her to be around at any time in the evening for work without liaising over a specific time to discuss something. Cheryl also immediately booked out holiday time at different points over the next year in her calendar. She was determined to take her holiday leave entitlement for a change, something she'd neglected in the past. Taking breaks would give her some much-needed holiday time to relax with Andrew.

Applying other strategies. Cheryl tried the advice from the quiz above and found she had particularly good results when she decided to let go of her rigid, habitual ways of doing things around the office, as well as becoming more flexible about her plans with Andrew. Certainly it helped that she'd decided she was going to spend less time at work in the evenings anyway, and that left her feeling freer and more confident to be open-minded to changes in their plans.

Replacing emotional habitual responses. The other element she made a note of in her diary was her negative emotional habitual responses. The one she could define most easily was when Andrew would sound 'laid back' about something like plans they were making. He would start to say something such as, 'You know, I'm not really bothered if we see Lisa and Nick next weekend or the weekend after,' and she'd feel her hackles rise immediately. She realised that when Andrew started to sound chilled out about something she'd feel the responsibility fall on her shoulders to sort out a definite plan. It was just 'one more thing for me to sort out' in her mind. Cheryl needed to turn her emotional habitual response 180 degrees onto its head and immediately seize hold of the opposing emotion to her anger and stress. She focused on learning to feel spontaneously chilled out and relaxed. At random points during the day she was to stop for a moment, close her eyes and recall a situation where she'd felt very relaxed. She was to encapsulate that feeling and hold onto it for a few moments. As this became more natural to Cheryl she found it easier to introduce this feeling at moments when she was confronted by her old habitual emotional feeling of anger and stress. Over a few months Cheryl's situation greatly improved and she reported that she was much happier and content in her life – both the professional and personal sides.

Habit evaluation exercise

In order to evaluate how much habits dictate your life in a negative way, commit to going through the following steps.

1. Dedicate one day to making a note of habitual responses – both practical and emotional. I don't mean things as basic as your waking-up and breakfast routines – unless of course they cause friction with a partner, flatmate or family members. Instead I mean those habitual responses that stand out to you as perhaps being too rigid (think of Cheryl's story), or that have been commented on by others, or that you know for a fact cause some sort of stress and strain, and influence your levels of happiness.

2. To make analysis easier you could use a separate sheet of paper for each, or use two pens of different colours and dedicate one to making notes on emotional habitual responses and the other to making notes on practical habitual responses.

3. Your notes should include:
    ♦ when you did or felt the habitual behaviour or response (remember, emotional habitual responses may simply be a *feeling* that wells up in you automatically),
    ♦ what it was in response to, and
    ♦ what the outcome was on your well-being, happiness or unhappiness.

    Some people who have extremely busy days find it more helpful to talk into a dictaphone as they make their habitual responses rather than writing them down in note form. Use whatever system works best for your lifestyle.

4. When it comes to the analysis there are two key things to look for:
    ♦ how your well-being or happiness level is affected, and
    ♦ how others might be affected by your habitual responses.

The reason why this is important is because, as mentioned earlier in *Happy Human*, responses to others and their responses back to us can establish a negative or positive cycle of relating and behaving to each other. Ultimately these cycles impact on our happiness.

5. Think about why you have begun to habitually respond in a particular way, and whether it comes from within you or in response to someone in your life. For instance, it may be that your partner actually does drag their feet and is always late, and you habitually respond by seeing red and shrieking at them. Or it might be that you have some impulse to behave in a certain way that's developed over the years and now needs changing.

6. Get creative and think of alternative ways to respond and behave. For instance, picture your enraged or stress reaction as part of a comedy sketch. Think how funny it would look if actually it wasn't sad. Practise this or any other alternative way of responding. Then initiate using them in the particular context where they'll be helpful to changing your habitual responses.

7. Definitely give yourself a pat on the back for making positive changes to habitual patterns.

Happiness Principle Nine

You do not have to be a slave to your habitual emotional and practical responses. You have the power to alter and change these to improve your well-being and increase opportunities for happiness.

When you learn to recognise habitual responses and behaviours that have a negative impact on your life you can also learn to substitute more positive ways of feeling, behaving and responding. You can break bad emotional and practical habits and substitute good ones in their place.

Boredom – the unacknowledged happiness wrecker

There's a silent enemy that lurks within your habitual responses and patterns of behaviour in your daily life. That silent enemy is boredom. It can gradually eat away at and diminish your experience of happiness without you even realising it.

It's easy to forget that we're naturally curious as human beings. Otherwise we wouldn't have undergone the amazing evolutionary changes that we have. Certainly during childhood we expand our horizons rapidly through our curiosity about the world. You can witness such curiosity at full throttle as you watch a young child, with their absolute drive to pick up, look at, feel and even taste, practically everything in their environment, as well as asking questions about everything around them, frequently to the point of driving their parents to distraction with their 'why' questions – Why does this or that happen? Why is that so big? Why is that so small? And so on!

But it's all too easy as adults to neglect this part of our nature, forgetting that we need to stimulate our curiosity from time to time. We get bogged down by our routines and can develop a type of 'wakeful sleepwalking'. Life passes you by and you suddenly realise that it's become very dull. This is a real problem for many people.

Stop being a slave to your television and other dull routines

The first step for combating boredom is to identify those routines in your life that directly lead to it. A big culprit is how much television people watch. American adults watch on average 28 hours per week compared to the slightly lower British average of about 27 hours per week.[38] That's staggering when you think about it – four hours a day of watching television. All that time to sit passively, being spoon-fed a diet of programmes ranging from the worthy to the terrible. I love a good drama, and other programmes, but would resist spending that many hours of my day sitting watching television.

Research repeatedly shows that those who spend less time sprawled in front of the TV are more connected to others and enjoy life more. Usually because they talk to them more – they sit and face them in conversation or in doing an activity together, rather than sitting and facing the TV. They feel greater happiness and fulfilment. Some tips to try and lessen your TV viewing include:

♦ Consider recording your absolute favourite programmes but otherwise give up that brain-numbing soap opera or B-list, late-night movies that you waste your time watching.
♦ Downsize the number of televisions in your home.
♦ Definitely remove them from your children's bedrooms despite their protests. Certainly no child under the age of 16 should have a TV in their bedroom. You'd be surprised how once they kick the TV habit they get interested in other things.

People have told me how once they put the vast hours they used to spend watching TV into enjoying their families instead, it made a tremendous difference to their lives. As well as simply enjoying more conversation, games or other hobbies, they'd get out for walks together, cook some real food rather than rely on ready-made meals, and treat themselves to simple pleasures like soaking longer in a lovely bubbly bath.

Why not take this as a golden opportunity to give up other dull routines and replace them with pleasurable things that improve your well-being? For instance, do you always iron on Saturday afternoons when your children are raring to run around the park? Reschedule the ironing for a time they're not around and instead enjoy getting out with them. Or do what I do and buy as many iron-free clothes as possible so you're not chained to your iron when there's life to be lived. A little imagination on your part can go a long way to uplifting your routine and giving you new moments of happiness.

 HAPPY FACT: *A simple smile releases feel-good brain chemicals – as well as looking attractive to others – so get smiling and learn to smile more freely and easily.*

Tap into your natural creativity

If you're like most adults you have probably lost touch with your natural creativity. It's so easy to do when life and all its necessary habits and routines seem to get in the way. However, it's terribly important to carve out time to pursue an interest or hobby that allows you a little creative expression or to stimulate your mind in another way. In fact simply taking up a new hobby has been found by research in America to be one key factor in a person's level of happiness.[39] I'm absolutely convinced that part of this happiness comes from committing time to doing something *for yourself* that you enjoy. It means you cherish yourself enough to allow yourself the time for developing and enjoying something that enriches your life.

This research also found that, when you become immersed and engrossed in pleasurable activities like a hobby, your cares and worries drift by the wayside. There's plenty of time to worry about things outside of your hobby-time!

The undiscovered power of your body clock

As I've said, we are creatures of habit. Some of these habits and habitual responses are absolutely fine and help streamline our lives, whereas others are negative and even destructive to our potential happiness. Have you ever thought about the implications of, say, that habitual impulse to sleep at night or that habitual sleepiness you feel after lunch? Or what about that energy surge you find you have at a certain point during the day that is not about forcing yourself to drink gallons of coffee?

These feelings and responses are influenced by an interesting source that feeds into the habits of our lifestyles – our body clocks. They have a part to play in getting us through the day and night that we usually fail to consider. The fascinating thing is that getting to know your unique and natural body-clock rhythms has implications for your well-being. One survey asked respondents about when they had their 'Eureka moments' – you know those moments, where suddenly you have a great idea or feel particularly switched-on or creative – and it found that many people have a natural creative surge at around 10 p.m., and they experience more creative moments in mid-evening than at other times.[40] So when it comes to changing dull routines, why not put that creativity to use in a way that stimulates and enriches your life, rather than falling onto the sofa in front of the TV mid-evening?

Other body-clock research confirms that there are variations between individuals that are important to pay attention to, because they influence how you feel during the day, and whether, say, you're an 'owl' or a 'lark' when it comes to doing your best work. A natural owl is someone who is a bit of a night person and is more productive later in the day, whereas a lark is a natural early bird. You might think this doesn't affect your well-being, but trust me, it does. I've known people that have been deeply unhappy in their work because they've been forced to rise early for a profession that requires it, when actually they're at their very best much later in the day. I've known people unhappy in day jobs to end up in the entertainment industry working in nightclubs, for example, and flourishing. Likewise I've known people in the nursing and medical professions who have found that when they change their work shifts, in one direction or another, they're happier at work. By exploring other occupations, or other companies that allow flexitime, you may find you alter the way you view your work. That's terribly important when it comes to how unhappy you might be feeling about your work routine. Understanding your natural body clock and how it works can help you to transform some unhappiness into feeling happier by working with your unique body rhythms, rather than against them.

Other in-depth research into how our bodies work and respond over a 24-hour period, and how we can optimise these responses, raises another interesting question when it comes to our habits.[41] Let's take having a workout. Many people like to get to the gym first thing in the morning before they go to work. However this research found that when many changed their workout habits to mid-afternoon, they optimised the benefits of exercise. A mid-afternoon workout led to improved blood pressure results and other positive changes. Also when it came to being able to concentrate on your work, this research found that late morning was the optimal time for many people.

Of course such findings apply to all of our lives and we need to think through how we can optimise the way we use our time. Let's say that you have a habit of scheduling *routine* meetings in the late morning, when actually your brain could be put to better use by scheduling more challenging meetings, or work, at that time. It's definitely worthwhile keeping at least a mental note, if not a proper diary, of the way you feel at different points of the day and evening. Use this information to optimise your performance in various aspects of your life.

OCD – when habits run out of control

You might wonder why I'm including a passage on obsessive compulsive order (OCD) when only about 4 per cent of the population has full-blown OCD. That's because although they may not have full-blown OCD, certainly a vast number of people have obsessive-compulsive *tendencies*. These can be soul-destroying, slowly chipping away at your well-being and *definitely* affecting your day-to-day happiness.

Let's begin with a brief description of OCD. It's a fear-based disorder where a person feels that they can't resist their obsessions and compulsions. We talked about facing the fears that affect your happiness, in a different context to OCD, in Chapter Seven. You can think of an obsession as an intrusive and repetitive *thought*. The content varies from worrying about something like picking up germs to fearing you'll actually do something 'bad' in public like swear, strip off or collapse. Obsessive thoughts can be about anything and everything. Most people tend to obsess over one particular area of their life, like cleanliness, or an aspect about themselves, their work or relationships, or something like safety, but of course you can have obsessive tendencies across any of your thinking. Your obsessions can impact your well-being in many ways, including:

♦ taking up your time
♦ using up your energy
♦ ensuring that you miss out on positive things
♦ affecting your self-esteem or self-belief because they eat away at areas of your life
♦ leading you to behave in negative or destructive ways.

That last point leads me to what a compulsion is. A compulsion is repetitive *behaviour* (rather than repetitive *thinking* as with obsessions) that you feel compelled to do in order to 'ward off' obsessive thoughts. So, for example, if you wash your hands five times (the compulsive behaviour), your obsessions (the thoughts) about germs are banished. If a full-blown OCD sufferer, and even someone with obsessive tendencies, can't carry out their ritual, it causes them distress of varying degrees. They're left with their obsessive thoughts whizzing around their head with no release through the compulsive behaviour that's been prevented.

You might have obsessive thinking or thoughts without any compulsive behaviour, or without *obvious* compulsive behaviour (it might not be obvious to you that you do certain things in relation to obsessive thoughts). But your obsessive thinking, alone, can be disturbing to your well-being and happiness.

I have a little theory about obsessive-compulsive behaviours. And that's that in ancient men and women, obsessive-compulsive behaviours were a positive thing. It was the man who repeatedly attempted to catch a certain animal – and finally succeeded – who was the one that devised the most successful hunting methods. It was the woman who repeatedly tended an area of ground who eventually developed a gardening method. And so on. It's my belief that such behaviours would have benefited our evolution, at least to a certain point, and that's why so many of the population have these tendencies now – these tendencies have been left in our genetic heritage. However, with the way our lives are now, these tendencies tend to be negative unless there's a specific benefit to, say, a particular occupation where you need to be obsessive – 'fine watchmaking' springs to mind, of all things! When you think holistically, and remember the fact that happiness and contentment don't normally come solely from your work, even those with obsessive tendencies that benefit their work may find these tendencies cause distress or unhappiness in other aspects of their life.

Do obsessions and/or compulsions dominate your life?

Answer these questions honestly to gauge whether any obsessive compulsive behaviours interfere with your happiness:

1. Do you find that you get 'locked' into a certain set of thoughts about something that you find very hard to shake off?

        Yes   No

2. Do you have little rituals or routines that you 'must do', like washing your hands in a particular way or arranging things 'just so'?

        Yes   No

3. Do you feel unnerved, upset, distressed, or generally unhappy if you can't carry out a little ritual or routine?

        Yes   No

4. Do you keep any obsessive-type thinking or compulsive behaviours secret from others?

        Yes   No

5. Do you feel happier, released from stress, simply 'better', when you can do your little rituals and routines?

        Yes   No

Your responses

If you answered 'Yes' to any of the above questions, you need to challenge what you're doing or thinking:

♦ First, because it may well be draining you emotionally and impacting on your well-being.

♦ Second, because any obsessive thinking or compulsive behaviours can spin out of control, particularly when you are faced with stress, and worsen. I've known people who think that their 'little ways' won't get any worse – and so they're OK to do or think them – until they're faced with something like a divorce or a bereavement, and then they get sent into a spin.

♦ Third, because certain behaviours are just downright bad for you, like a woman I recently met whose repeated, vigorous hand-washing led to terrible eczema. I know of cases of people making themselves ill by taking huge levels of vitamins, convinced they'll get some terrible disease if they don't. And a compulsive use of cleaning fluids, to keep a home superclean, can set off asthma.

Seven steps to solve obsessive compulsive habits

Follow these seven steps to decrease any obsessive compulsive habits you may have and increase your levels of happiness.

Step 1: Explore where your obsessive compulsive habits come from. Are they fuelled by some sort of fear or anxiety? Perhaps your parent or parents had OCD and you learnt that life's frightening and you must 'control' the fear with certain behaviours. Or you might have experienced a trauma, and obsessive compulsive habits became your way of 'coping' in the aftermath. Maybe it's the way you react when demands mount at work or at home. Understanding this gives you more power and a springboard for action.

Step 2: Begin by keeping an obsessive compulsive habits diary for one week. Make it simple – mark a *tick* for each obsessive thought that you have and a *cross* for each compulsive behaviour. Briefly note any 'trigger' that sets off the thought or behaviour.

Step 3: Examine your diary for patterns. Can you determine what sets you off? For example, is it stress when you're rushing around and getting ready for work that leaves you fretful, so that you return to re-check the locks on your front door a couple of times after leaving for work? On a separate sheet write down:

♦ your main 'triggers' for obsessive compulsive habits (say, getting stressed by your morning routine before work),

♦ your obsessive or compulsive responses, and

♦ relevant goals, for example, to stop re-checking locks.

Step 4: Before implementing any strategy, begin to 'reframe' your thinking. Accept that obsessive compulsive habits are NOT a positive and happy coping strategy. Up until now you may have seen them as your coping mechanism, your saviour even! But they are the opposite, preventing you from learning positive coping strategies. Headline your piece of paper from Step 3 with the fact 'My obsessive compulsive habits are not coping strategies!' Hold this thought.

Step 5: Now you should enlist loved ones to help you with your action plan. If you share your life with a partner, close friends or family members, their support can be vital in resisting your obsessive compulsive habits. Explain clearly to them what you've identified through your diary and how you're planning to change this. Tell them you need support in moving forward.

Step 6: Taking action requires a number of elements.

♦ Select your first goal. For example, if you wash your hands twice whenever you touch food, the goal is to resist and wash once only.

♦ As you resist the urge to wash again, use deep breathing to relax your body.

♦ Also use continual communication with a loved one about your feelings of fear. Report to them *out loud* how you're feeling while you resist that extra hand-washing.

♦ Now affirm to yourself that nothing bad has happened and that you've coped despite not carrying out your compulsive behaviour.
♦ Give yourself loads of praise for your resistance and acknowledge that setting goals and good communication are positive coping strategies.

Step 7: Continue to monitor your goals and stress levels. Let's say that you have three key rituals to tackle – one at a time – building your coping-confidence. Prioritise them and perhaps start by challenging yourself over the simplest one first. Keep an open dialogue with loved ones about your successes and your failures. Don't become secretive about obsessive compulsive habits when it comes to the thoughts and behaviours that you fail to resist. Carry on being open-minded to implementing real coping strategies like talking about difficulties and looking for solutions to the stresses we all face. When you start to challenge and conquer these sorts of destructive habitual responses you'll feel your well-being and happiness increase. It's a wonderful thing to rise to such challenges.

I've now highlighted a number of ways in which habitual responses, whether practical or emotional, can either ease you through life or diminish your enjoyment of life. It's wise to remember that these are often habits of a lifetime and don't change overnight. Simply increasing your awareness of the way you habitually respond in your life can be an enormous benefit. When you go on to act to improve certain behaviours, or prevent others, you'll feel a sense of relief and release.

Now I'd like to explore the final Happiness Principle that has a frequently much under-estimated impact on your well-being, profoundly affecting your sense of unhappiness or happiness.

Build Your Happiness Habit

Throw caution to the wind every day and free yourself of one habitual response or routine – at least for that day.

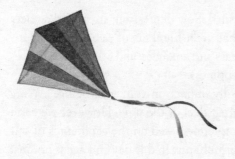

Modern Life and Your Happiness

> *If only we'd stop trying to be happy*
> *we'd have a pretty good time.*
> Edith Wharton

I hope you've now seen from the first nine Happiness Principles that there's a tremendous amount we can do to create more happiness in our lives as well as much that holds us back from being happy. My tenth Happiness Principle turns to the complicated times we live in: *how do they influence how happy or unhappy we are?*

It's hardly surprising that in these stressful times many people are unhappy, and rightly concerned about finding personal happiness amongst so many dark clouds. When you're worried about real, gritty issues like paying the bills and job security it's actually logical that statistics show depression, stress and anxiety have increased.[42] And that great numbers of people are experiencing low self-esteem, fears and anxieties, and other related issues that damage potential happiness.

These things profoundly impact on your well-being, leaving you feeling unhappy a great deal of the time. However we can't let our happiness be completely based on the economics of our lives. And being happy or unhappy in this day and age is not just a simple matter of economic woes. Look at the facts and you'll see that even in times of economic strength in recent decades, there have still been large numbers of people seeking treatment for stress and depression and all those other emotional states we associate with unhappiness. Research shows us that the last time we humans were supposedly a fairly happy, contented lot was back in the 1950s.[43]

In part that's one reason why I decided to write *Happy Human* – it's time for some understanding of why so many people are unhappy right now. What has changed in the last 50–60 years to have had such a negative impact on our well-being? I'm not gilding the 1950s as an ideal, golden time that we should hark back to. But understanding the vast changes we've undergone might go a long way in helping people embrace a happier lifestyle.

With that in mind I'd like to highlight themes, in brief, affecting every person. I say 'in brief' because I simply want them to stimulate some thought about how you live your life, plus *all that surrounds you*. You know I don't like avoidance and to avoid considering these themes jeopardises your chance of happiness. Simple reflection will benefit you and your life and that's why for each theme I ask you to put pen to paper in the simplest but hopefully most thought-provoking way.

The family tree

Our modern lifestyle with its emphasis on material wealth and fast pace has a lot to answer for. It doesn't sit well with our most basic human needs to be emotionally and socially connected in small and meaningful groups. I strongly believe this theme of positive family connection has suffered in recent years. The fracturing of the extended family definitely goes against our core nature.

It causes many of us deep and lasting unhappiness that we're physically and geographically separated from our initial blood-ties – our families, old friends and acquaintances. This leads us to feel disconnected from our roots. Just look at the success of television and radio programmes, as well as websites, that trace people's ancestry. And look at the huge success of websites that help you link up with old school friends. These confirm that we're dying to find out about our roots and to feel closer to our family ties and friends. I know from hearing the stories of thousands of people the profound and destructive effect that the breakdown of their family tree and friendships have had on their overall happiness.

Note here the last time you wished a loved one was closer at hand:

✎ ....

Money, money, money

Next comes a recurring theme in our modern lives where we're constantly being fed an aspirational diet of needing more 'stuff' to be successful and happy humans. Nothing could be further from the truth. As long as we have shelter, warmth, food, work, and so on, the last things we need are loads of material things to clutter our very existence.

The ancient Greek philosopher Epicurus recognised this, proposing that the simple things in life like companionship, plus having the basic necessities like food and shelter, brought happiness. Research confirms that the things that make people most happy *aren't* material things – instead they're things that bring real quality to our lives, like love, family contentment, health and friendships. My travels around the world also confirm this, and have shown me time and time again that the people who live much more simple lives that aren't dominated by accumulating more 'stuff' are generally happier.[44]

Note here something you bought that you didn't need, that was a waste of your time going out to purchase it and/or a waste of your money:

 ....

Curiosity didn't kill the cat

Another important theme to consider affecting your happiness has to do with the fact that we're innately curious as human beings. I've mentioned stimulating your natural creativity and curiosity is part of this. With our curiosity comes the need to understand something new, and that in turn means we need *time* to understand. So when we're constantly bombarded with things like the updates in technology that surround us, they overwhelm us.

As curious beings we want to satisfy the urge to get to grips with these new things. Frequently I see people overwhelmed as the small and precious amount of time they have slips away as they spend time in this way. This also ties in with the pressure we're under to accumulate things – to aspire to have the latest mobile, palmtop, camera or whatever. You can easily see how what starts out as the pursuit of understanding and desiring or aspiring to own some new technology very quickly impinges on the happiness you might have been feeling *before* unwrapping that new mobile phone that ends up taking your entire evening to master. I know – I've been there! It's not even the time spent mastering, say, a new palmtop, but the hours and days lost when your internet server fails you or your PC gets a glitch. Remember the iconic piece of film of the man who threw his PC across his office? Such frustrated behaviour has been repeated in too many offices. Many people feel complete slaves to the technology that was supposed to help them.

Note here the last time you were frustrated by a piece of technology – how did it affect the way you felt?

 ....

The human kind of communication

Of course, there are many wonders of technology, and one of them is the instant communication provided by email, text messaging, 'tweeting' and so on. These have been a fabulous gift to both professional and personal aspects of our lives. However, there are limits to the benefits, and increasingly I hear from people who are overwhelmed by technological methods of communication. They feel driven to stay in contact 24/7. This goes completely against the essence of our humanity, where we were meant to have periods of quiet and even solitude. Time for reflection is important, as well as time to simply connect with only the most important people in our life – and not being bothered by others trying to contact us at any given time.

Ironically, being connected in this way 24/7 can lead you to feel detached from real communication. Despite its benefits, communication through technology can get in the way of voice-to-voice and/or face-to-face communication, which is terribly important to us as humans: we gain real comfort in actual contact with each other. This real contact has been jeopardised in people who become reliant on technological contact.

Note here the last time you felt put upon by your mobile or palmtop bleeping at you, perhaps interfering with a conversation you were having face-to-face:

All the hours God gave you

We're also torn apart further by the pressure and anxiety we have hanging over us if we don't give all our time to our job. In the shrinking, competitive, short-contract job market of modern life we feel compelled to work longer and longer hours so that we're seen to be 'hard at it'. We hope this means we're less likely to be given the chop. Not only do we have a sense of having to perform well in our job for long hours, but this feeling is made even worse by those very long hours we then do. They exhaust and drain us, disconnecting us even further from what we enjoy in life and interfering with our relationships.

Note here the last time you felt exhausted by work or that your work had taken over your life:

Vacancy for a role model

I'd like you to take a moment to ask yourself who you look up to. Who is your role model? It might be that you simply don't have one. In generations past, people could quickly identify their role models, but this is no longer the case. This is partly because over the last few decades we've gone through a sea change when it comes to things like fulfilling our own needs and putting ourselves first, rather than looking towards a role model for our beliefs, ideals and how to lead our lives.

Of course autonomy, independence and fulfilling our needs is a good thing, but none of us has all the answers. Also in many ways we've gone too far and developed a 'me, me, me' society. There seems to be hardly anyone to aspire to, someone who sets a good example for us through qualities like sacrifice, creativity, doing good things for others and being altruistic. Sadly many aspire to the rather hollow lives that famous people lead in our celebrity-obsessed culture. They desire the clothing of their favourite pop star and look up to a celebrity's sense of style. They might even look up to them as a role model, thinking that somehow this person who lives in the public eye is 'good' simply for being photographed. As role models, celebrities usually only provide shallow values around things like material acquisition – the expensive clothes, cars and lifestyle. The politically interested George Clooneys, and those motivated by a cause like the Richard Geres of this world, are rare.

Also at the most basic level it's a fact that fashion and pop music tastes change as frequently as a revolving door, and so if your role model is a pop star or fashion icon, then by definition they won't last. What we really need, deep down in our human heart, is to look up to something enduring that gives a sense of constancy, and that is something positive, that you can strive to be like in your world. We only need to consider our ancient ancestors, and how every culture had something they idolised, like nature and Mother Earth, or selected a leader who was actually a role model, to see that this is an enduring part of our psyche. However with the exception (at the time of writing) of the new President Obama, the vast majority of role models we are fed by the media in the form of celebrity worship are often shallow and empty.

Note here who you admire and why you admire them:

....

Spirituality

This brings me nicely to spirituality and belief systems, which initially evolved to bring people hope and a sense that they could celebrate something important together. Throughout the millennia humans have bonded in this way through sacred, spiritual and religious beliefs. Whether you're religious or not, I think you might agree that many people don't feel bonded to others in this way any more. For many this means they experience a certain emptiness when it comes to their lack of spirituality. And with that emptiness comes a longing to feel something – anything – so they end up trying to fill the emptiness. As with filling a painful emotional hole, covered in Chapter Five, what do people tend to fill such spiritual emptiness with? This void may be filled by damaging pursuits that are destructive to happiness like excessive drinking, drug-taking and sex, when the person actually wants love, for example.

Note here if you have any special beliefs or spirituality, and how they enrich your life, or not, as the case may be:

....

Ask for nothing in return

A lack of spirituality, and a sense that you have nothing and no one to look up to, is part of a more general emotional poverty in our society. The fact that we have little time, as we work all hours to get the 'stuff' that we think we need, leaves even less time to be community-spirited. It's rare that we do something for another person and ask, or expect, nothing in return. We feel too drained and time-short to worry about showing simple kindnesses to others. Good things that help prevent emotional poverty like volunteering, and generally making sure your immediate community (and even the larger community) is OK, are neglected. This state of affairs – where your potential to have real emotional wealth and happiness is chipped away at, piece by piece – can be nearly as destructive as actual poverty.

Note here the last time you did something for an individual or for your community just for the sake of it:

✎ ....

It wasn't meant to be this way

Another theme that definitely affects our well-being and underlies unhappiness is the fact that as humans we were not meant to be tucked into little 'boxes' in our work place. Our ancient ancestors roamed the land and had plenty of opportunity to take natural exercise. Our modern lifestyle completely goes against the grain, turning many of us into desk-slaves and couch potatoes when we were meant to stretch our limbs and fill our lungs with fresh air. We were also intended to enjoy a varied, nutritious and 'organic' diet. In our fast-living and fast-food culture these basic needs simply aren't being met.

Note here the last time you had a healthy meal or got out for fresh air:

✎ ....

The young ones

If you're a parent and/or someone that's concerned with young people, an important theme to the backdrop to our levels of happiness concerns children and young people. Having worked in this field I honestly don't think on the whole they're loved and cherished enough in our society. This is a very different matter to giving children their 'rights' as they've received them over the last decade or so. Instead it's about the way we live and how it simply doesn't leave enough time or energy to nurture young people the way they deserve.

We've also allowed huge pressures to build up on young people to grow up too quickly. They're freely influenced by the things they should be protected from, like unsuitable violence and access to pornography on the internet and their mobile phones. They're clearly not protected from advertising, which encourages materialistic consumption, they're overly concerned with their appearance, influenced by the shallowness of celebrity, and generally not raised with enough love and care.[45] And this means they actually miss out on key life experiences of simple, youthful enjoyment of the world around them and deep and profound love and nurturing.

If you're a parent or responsible for young people – perhaps you're a teacher – please note here the last time you gave consideration to these issues and whether or not they concern you:

Instant gratification

There's one further theme I'd like to mention that has a profound effect on our levels of happiness, particularly when it comes to our relationships. This is the instant gratification culture pervading every aspect of lives. Yes, it's convenient to order a pizza and have it delivered to your doorstep in 20 minutes. And to shop on the internet often saves time trudging around the shops. However our expectations that everything happens quickly has an insidious effect on the aspects of our lives that don't necessarily have instant solutions, instant success or instant gratification. The fact that many people find their relationships – the absolute glue of society generally and personal happiness specifically – unsatisfactory is due to unrealistic expectations that things should be romantic and wonderful, and after there's a disagreement, instantly 'OK' again. These expectations are unreasonable and unachievable, yet they hang over our relationships, our professional expectations, and everything else we do.

Have you recently found yourself impatient over something that in actual fact required a little more thought, time, or energy?

 ....

Happiness Principle Ten

Develop your awareness of the world around you and don't underestimate how it affects you and your happiness.

Our modern lifestyles have a profound effect on us, and you need to set boundaries on how much you buy into some aspects of contemporary life. You can find the personal strength to say 'No' to things in our environment and modern culture that take away from your quality of life.

Stop pursuing 'stuff'

I'd like to get you focused on ridding yourself of the pursuit of more 'stuff'. The average household is literally stuffed with gadgets and ornaments. Some are rarely or never used. What a waste! This is why we've many negative sayings about money, such as, 'Money can't buy you love', 'Money is the root of all evil', and 'Money often costs too much'. Wisdom has taught us that true happiness doesn't have a price tag.[46] Your happiness is not dependent on material wealth. You might work yourself silly so that you can buy the next must-have item. But you may well find you don't have time to enjoy these things and suffer emotional and physical stress pursuing them.

So I'd like you to plan over the next four weekends to choose a few items to give to charity shops. Once you start clearing cupboards some of your purchases seem wasteful and you might wonder why you started accumulating these things. Next, think before you buy something. Have a 48-hour window before buying. Work out the time it takes you to get to the shop, search for the item, stand in the queue to pay, and then get home – add all those minutes and half-hours up – you'll be surprised how even a simple purchase can take ages. Spend that time with someone you love and forget the latest gizmo.

You could also start to consider the themes running through your life that truly influence your levels of happiness. It would be worth your while to simply mull over questions like: 'Am I too concerned with acquiring stuff?' Your answers might get you thinking that there's a different way to live.

 HAPPY FACT: *Relationship research shows that remembering happy events by looking at old photographs strengthens your love.*

Be careful what you wish for

If you haven't already got enough food for thought about our modern lifestyles, then you should also be careful what you wish for. I've spoken to countless people who thought they *really wished* for that promotion, or they *really wished* they'd get that new job with more responsibility, for example, only to find it wasn't what they expected once they were there. In fact they felt worse, because with those new responsibilities, expectations and aspirations came even more stress and pressure. There are many benefits to aspiring to do something better in your work. There's absolutely nothing wrong with hopes and dreams and aspirations. And being competitive in your work can be a positive thing. However these things always have to be *in balance* with what you 'pay' both emotionally, and in terms of your energy, to get there.

I've now briefly highlighted a number of themes that truly impact on human happiness and it's certainly not an exhaustive list. But I've included the ones I think we ignore at our cost. I'm absolutely convinced that most or even all of these themes run through *your life* as they do through other people's lives. If you allow some time to reflect on these themes, and also allow your thoughts about them to serve as a backdrop to the other nine Happiness Principles, then this will help you take a holistic approach to embracing more happiness in your life. Now, it's time for your happy beginning.

Build Your Happiness Habit

Today and every day, check yourself, and be aware of how the demands of the world around you influence your well-being and happiness.

Conclusion

This is Your Happy Beginning . . .

*The time to be happy is now. The place to
be happy is here. The way to be happy is
to make others so.*

Anonymous

I've now described the 10 Happiness Principles. I like to think of this as the beginning of a fresh journey where you embrace these principles, as and when they apply to your unique life. Some will come into play immediately as you've recognised your experiences, thoughts and feelings in particular passages – and seen what you can now do to change or enhance them to optimise your happiness. Others may help you embrace more happiness in the future and understand any unhappiness when it touches your life.

Thinking of the 10 Happiness Principles and how they may play in and out of your life, my life, and everyone else's lives, brings me back to that question we all ask – *what do humans need to be happy?*

♦ From our own individual perspectives we need to stop blaming others for how we feel, and accept that when another person brings unhappiness into our lives, we'll set boundaries on their behaviour.

♦ We need to take responsibility for ourselves and our lives, as well as learning to listen to our intuition about all sorts of matters.

♦ We need to love and care for ourselves enough to learn what makes us happy and how to bring more of this happiness into our lives.

♦ We need to be clear that we're living our own life, on our terms, but with respect, care and love for others.

♦ We need to recognise any emotional hole that we attempt to fill in unhappy ways, challenge those unhelpful habits that jeopardise our happiness, and face the fears that cause unhappiness.

♦ We need to understand and enhance our relationships, give love and receive it, dare to trust others and ourselves, and learn from hurdles in our relationships.

♦ We need to reach high for our dreams but also learn that happiness can be very simple when we sit back and enjoy the little pleasures and tiny joys, seize those elusive moments that might provide a bit of magic, and grab fresh opportunities, too.

♦ And we need to understand the whirling dervish of a world surrounding us and how it impacts on our well-being.

Day by day, if you can strive for these things, you *will* become a happy human. Being a happy human also means accepting that unhappiness is a part of life. That you'll find solutions where you can, accept where things are beyond your control, and know that happiness can be yours again across the smaller picture and the bigger picture.

Identifying your happiness-unhappiness behaviours

Make a list here of at least three happiness-*increasing* behaviours of yours, for instance, making a point of regularly chatting to a best friend:

 ....

Now make a note of at least three happiness-*decreasing* behaviours of yours, for instance, not daring to speak up for fear of rejection:

 ....

You have the power to keep identifying the behaviours and expectations that bring love, respect, confidence, well-being and happiness to you. You can bring the 'three Es' – *good* **emotions**, **experiences** and **energy** – into your life.

Happiness can sometimes feel like an elusive goal when you've taken a knock, faced heartbreak, or had the emotional stuffing knocked out of you. In the face of profound unhappiness, research shows it can literally lead to 'heartache'.[47] But happiness is not elusive, and if you search for the smallest glimmer, the little joy, that touch of courage, it'll come to you.

Answer the ultimate question

Here's one last thought-provoking question for you. Answer this *honestly*: if you died tomorrow what would you have changed about the last week of your life? Unfortunately many of us coast through life believing we're *always* going to be around. Those I've met who had 'wake-up calls', such as surviving a serious car accident or a brain tumour operation, are the ones who really appreciate the short life we have.

Count your blessings every day. Write them down where you'll see them – in your desk diary or on the kitchen pad. Those people who have had life-threatening ordeals are those most likely to realise that life's pretty darned great. You may never get a wake-up call, so don't wait until it's too late to make the most of what you have.

And now it's time to remind you in full of the 10 Happiness Principles to live your life by.

Happiness Principle One

Regardless of your upbringing you have the power to choose to find happiness.

In other words your happiness is shaped by the way you were raised – but that doesn't mean you can't change it. We are not slaves to our childhoods. However, it's important to understand how the echoes from our childhoods reach forward throughout our lives – sometimes in the most profound ways.

Happiness Principle Two

Find the 'likeable' in you, as once you discover it you'll go from strength to strength.

When you like yourself, you'll make sure you bring good emotions, experiences and energy (the three Es) into your life, you'll do more of what you like, and you'll come to love yourself. And that means finding more happiness.

Happiness Principle Three

Take control of your life and you give yourself every opportunity to find what makes you happy.

When you feel in charge it can be exhilarating and daunting in equal measure. But when you decide you'll attempt to control or face what daunts you, you can take your life in the direction you wish. Along the way it can at times be an exciting journey, and in facing life this way you'll enjoy many rewards.

Happiness Principle Four

Learn to embrace happiness on a smaller scale and it can increase happiness in the bigger picture.

It's often easier to start small – and think about increasing your Smaller Picture Happiness – than to worry about the big picture, as that can seem overwhelming at times. Taking little steps to enjoy unexpected moments of pleasure and joy can go a long way to improving all the strands of your life.

Happiness Principle Five

It's important to accept that you are only human and to be human is to experience emotional pain. Learn to recognise any pain that exists within you and don't run from it.

You can slowly heal any emotional hole inside of you. Don't fool yourself that you're abnormal or different from others because of your pain. You are *not* different and you are *not* alone.

Happiness Principle Six

Your relationships with others are crucial to your happiness. Nurture and care for them and expect to be treated as you treat others.

Your relationships have the power to enhance you and your happiness and/or bring you unhappiness. But it goes both ways and you affect those you relate with in a profound way too.

Happiness Principle Seven

You can become fearless as it's within your power. At some point in your life you became fearful but you weren't born that way.

Ultimately you can free yourself from fear. You don't have to live a life of fear, anxiety and worry – instead you can face changing circumstances, difficulties and hurdles with courage.

Happiness Principle Eight

When you develop and embrace the power of your intuition, you deepen your self-belief, which in turn brings you more happiness.

Belief in your intuition is ultimately a belief in your deepest self that embraces all of your senses. When you attain that level of self-belief you develop a greater understanding of the world around you and of your life. That means you can enhance those things that make you happy.

Happiness Principle Nine

You do not have to be a slave to your habitual emotional and practical responses. You have the power to alter and change these to improve your well-being and increase opportunities for happiness.

When you learn to recognise habitual responses and behaviours that have a negative impact on your life you can also learn to substitute more positive ways of feeling, behaving and responding. You can break bad emotional and practical habits and substitute good ones in their place.

Happiness Principle Ten

Develop your awareness of the world around you and how it affects you and your happiness.

Our modern lifestyles have a profound effect on us and you need to set boundaries on how much you buy into it. You can find the personal strength to say 'No' to things in our environment and modern culture that take away from your quality of life.

Good luck, love, and enjoy a happy beginning from me! Dr Pam x

References

1 Mental Health Foundation, January 2009.
2 2006, BBC Radio 2. As part of a six-part series, Science of Happiness, the BBC compared contemporary statistics with a Gallup poll from 1957, finding that far more people in the 1950s reported themselves as happy with their lives.
3 Prof Martin Seligman *et al* (2005), 'Positive Psychology Progress: An Empirical Validation Of Interventions' in *American Psychologist*, July–August. Plus various research.
4 Dr Alexander Weiss, University of Edinburgh, research on genetics, happiness and well-being published in *Psychological Science*, March 2008.
5 Prof Walter Mischel, Stanford University, California: research from the Bing Nursery School studies in the 1960s, following this cohort through early adulthood.
6 Dr Patricia Koch, Penn State University: research into female sexual desire, loss of libido, body image and self-esteem (various research).

6 Children's Society Report, February 2009, 'A Good
   Childhood: Searching for Values in a Competitive Age'.
7 Survey conducted by Gumtree.com
8 Dr Daniel Nettle, University of Newcastle: conference at the
   University of Teesside in July 2008, 'More than pleasure, less
   than virtue: getting a grip on happiness' (and various
   research).
9 Richard Layard (2005) *Happiness: Lessons from a New
   Science*, Penguin. And (2006) 'Happiness and Public Policy'
   in *Economic Journal*, 116, C24-C33. And (2003) Lionel
   Robbins Memorial Lectures, 3rd, 4th and 5th March.
10 Prof. Ruut Veenhoven (2006), 'Healthy Happiness – effects
   of happiness on physical health and the consequences for
   preventive health care' *Journal of Happiness Studies.*
11 Eric Weiner, *The Geography of Bliss*, 2008.
12 Dr Richard Tunney, University of Nottingham, report
   commissioned by the National Lottery: Happiness Comes
   Cheap – Even from Millionaires, October 2007.
13 Kerri Cartwright, lottery winner in 2007, quoted in the *Daily
   Mail*, October 2007.
14 Dr William Bird, University of Portsmouth, 2006, 'Walking
   for Health'.
15 *Woman and Home* magazine survey, August 2008.
16 James Montier, *Psychology of Banking Report 2005*.
17 David G. Blanchflower and Andrew J. Oswald (2007)
   'Hypertension and Happiness across Nations' IZA
   discussion paper number 2633 *American Journal of
   Hypertension*.
18 Dr Atilla Szabo, Nottingham Trent University, various work
   on the impact of television on well-being.
19 Survey by Netmums, 2006.
20 Mental Health Foundation study, 2007.

21 Dr Paul Keedwell (2008), *How Sadness Survived: the evolutionary basis of depression*, Radcliffe Publishing Ltd.

22 Prof Jerome Wakefield (2009), 'The Loss of Sadness: Are We Misdiagnosing Normal Human Emotion as Clinical Depression?' in the Lindemann Lecture in Human Development at Adelphi's Ruth S. Harley University Center, 1 South Avenue, Garden City, NY.

23 Drs James Gross & Jane Richards, *New Scientist*, 2005.

24 2008 statistics from The Office of National Statistics.

25 Foundation for Mental Health Care, Delft, Holland, 2007.

26 Prof Ed Diener (2009), *The Collected Works of Ed Diener*, Springer

27 J. Holt-Lunstad, W. Birmingham and B.G. Jones (2008), 'Is There Something Unique about Marriage? The relative impact of marital status, relationship quality and network social support on ambulatory blood pressure and mental health' in *Annals of Behavioural Medicine*, April 2008.

28 Prof C. Dush, M. Taylor and R. Kroeger (2008) 'Marital Happiness and Psychological Well-Being Across the Life Course'; in *Family Relations*, April.

29 Prof Ray Pahl (2000), *On Friendship*, Polity.

30 Prof John Cacioppo, University of Chicago, presented research at the American Association for the Advancement of Science annual conference, February 2009.

31 Prof. Martin Seligman (2006), *Learned Optimism: How to Change Your Mind and Your Life*, Vintage Books.

32 *National Geographic* survey of phobias published 2007.

33 Prof Ken Paller (2007), 'Subliminal Smells Can Guide Social Preferences' in *Journal of Psychological Science*, December 2007.

34 Prof A. Dijksterhuis (2006), 'Think different: The role of unconscious and conscious processes in attitude formation

and decision-making', research talk presented at University of Amsterdam.

35 Prof. Andrew Clark and Dr Orsolya Leikes, research presented to the Royal Economic Society's annual conference, 2007.

36 Prof Michael Reveley, University of Leicester Medical School. The establishment of the Human Dolphin Therapy Centres arising from various research including randomised controlled trial of animal facilitated therapy with dolphins in the treatment of depression, in the British Medical Journal, November 2005, Prof Michael Reveley and Christian Antonioli.

37 British study of happiness that took place in Slough, Berks, 2005.

38 A. C. Nielsen report, 2008.

39 See note 3

40 Survey of 1,400 adults by hotel chain Crowne Plaza.

41 Prof. Russell Foster (2004), Rhythms of Life: The Biological Clocks That Control the Daily Lives of Every Living Thing, Yale University Press.

42 See note 1

43 See note 2

44 Dr Richard Tunney, University of Nottingham, School of Psychology, from a news article: 'They Are Rich Who Have True Friends', October, 2008.

45 See note 6

46 See note 9

47 Dr William Whang, Columbia University study, reported in March, 2009, issue of the Journal of the American College of Cardiology.